The Battle Behind the Wire

U.S. Prisoner and Detainee Operations from World War II to Iraq

T0302944

Cheryl Benard, Edward O'Connell,

Cathryn Quantic Thurston, Andres Villamizar,

Elvira N. Loredo, Thomas Sullivan, Jeremiah Goulka

Prepared for the Office of the Secretary of Defense

Approved for public release; distribution unlimited

 NATIONAL DEFENSE RESEARCH INSTITUTE

The research described in this report was prepared for the Office of the Secretary of Defense (OSD). The research was conducted within the RAND National Defense Research Institute, a federally funded research and development center sponsored by OSD, the Joint Staff, the Unified Combatant Commands, the Navy, the Marine Corps, the defense agencies, and the defense Intelligence Community under Contract W74V8H-06-C-0002.

Library of Congress Control Number: 2010942311

ISBN: 978-0-8330-5045-8

Published 2011 by the RAND Corporation
1776 Main Street, P.O. Box 2138, Santa Monica, CA 90407-2138
1200 South Hayes Street, Arlington, VA 22202-5050
4570 Fifth Avenue, Suite 600, Pittsburgh, PA 15213-2665
RAND URL: http://www.rand.org/
To order RAND documents or to obtain additional information, contact
Distribution Services: Telephone: (310) 451-7002;
Fax: (310) 451-6915; Email: order@rand.org

Preface

In major conflicts dating to World War II and continuing through recent operations in Iraq, U.S. forces have taken a large number of prisoners or detainees. Although prisoner of war (POW) and detainee operations ultimately tend to become quite extensive, military planners and policymakers have repeatedly treated such operations as an afterthought. In reality, such operations can be a central part of the successful prosecution of a conflict. Determining how to gain knowledge from, hold, question, influence, and release captured adversaries can be an important component of military strategy and doctrine, both during the conflict and in reconstruction afterward.

This publication presents a historical analysis of POW operations during World War II, the Korean War, and the Vietnam War, as well as detailed analyses of detainee operations during the recent conflict in Iraq. It should be of interest to military planners, strategists, and policymakers concerned with ongoing and future prisoner and detainee operations.

This research was sponsored by the Office of the Secretary of Defense and conducted within the International Security and Defense Policy Center of the RAND National Defense Research Institute, a federally funded research and development center sponsored by the Office of the Secretary of Defense, the Joint Staff, the Unified Combatant Commands, the Navy, the Marine Corps, the defense agencies, and the defense Intelligence Community.

For more information on the RAND International Security and Defense Policy Center, see http://www.rand.org/nsrd/ndri/centers/isdp.html or contact the director (contact information is provided on the web page).

Contents

Figures

Tables

Summary

In every major extended U.S. military action of the 20th century, including World War II, the Korean War, and the Vietnam War, U.S. forces have captured or detained a large number of combatants. While each conflict presented unique challenges, there are many common initial misjudgments on the part of U.S. forces regarding the size and character of the detention population. Lessons from this history of detention operations were not initially incorporated into detention operations that U.S. forces launched in Iraq and Afghanistan. Particularly lacking was guidance on the role of detention operations in counterinsurgencies. The Abu Ghraib prisoner abuse scandal and its successful use by insurgents in propaganda against the United States is a powerful example of how detention operations are not a coincidental product of a conflict but are a central part of shaping the ongoing counterinsurgency campaign and post-conflict outcomes.

In an effort to develop an updated, comprehensive strategy and doctrine on how best to conduct prisoner and detainee operations, Multi-National Force–Iraq (MNF-I) asked the RAND Corporation to analyze detainee operations over time. This monograph fulfills that request. It presents a historical overview of prisoner operations in World War II, Korea, and Vietnam. It provides a more-detailed overview of detainee operations in Iraq. Commanders in Iraq afforded RAND researchers unprecedented access in 2007 and 2008 to observe the management of detainee operations. This included observations at eight regional detainee handling areas as well as observations of special detainee populations, including juveniles, females, convicted criminals, and political refugees. This document also presents the unique top-level perspectives of three successive Task Force (TF) 134 commanders charged with overseeing Theater Internment Facility detainee operations in Iraq.

Historical Operations

World War II

POWs taken by Allied forces during World War II differ markedly from those taken in more-recent conflicts, particularly that in Iraq. Nevertheless, there are parallels between prisoner operations during World War II and those of subsequent conflicts, both in initial missteps and ultimate program goals.

The first misjudgment in handling German prisoners was underestimating the number of prisoners the Allies would take and their speed in capturing them. This meant the United States was unprepared for the scale of operations needed to administer a population that would approach a half-million. Once the German prisoners were taken, U.S. military authorities viewed them as a homogeneous grouping of Nazis. This allowed Nazi leadership to reassert itself within the camps to the detriment of the non-Nazi majority. Finally, U.S. policymakers were slow to realize that prisoners should not simply be warehoused and used to fill labor needs but that they provided an opportunity to help shape both the continuing conflict and postwar Europe.

U.S. policymakers ultimately provided education programs for German prisoners. These efforts were controversial at the time, given widespread beliefs—similar to some current ones about Iraqi insurgents—that soldiers of the Nazi regime would resist such education. Yet the programs succeeded in training several leaders of postwar Germany, inculcating in them positive feelings about both democracy and the United States.

The Korean War

Few lessons the United States learned in administering prisoner populations during World War II carried over to the Korean War. The

U.S. Army had quickly demobilized after World War II, and experienced soldiers returned to civilian life. As a result, in Korea, the Army and the United Nations Command faced many challenges managing prisoners, including a lack of qualified personnel, dependence on less-qualified South Korean guards, a lack of preconflict planning for handling massive numbers of prisoners, an inability to correctly identify political tendencies of prisoners, a failure to see influence of prisoners as part of the battle, and difficulty in applying principles from the new international conventions for handling prisoners.

U.S. forces took a large number of prisoners quickly. Shortly after the Inch'on landing, U.S. forces took nearly 100,000 prisoners, and tens of thousands more after the intervention of Chinese troops. These were housed at a few large camps, where prisoner control problems would recur.

The international law governing detention in time of war had been amended in the Geneva Conventions of 1949, but the United States did not ratify them until after the end of the war. The United States, and other countries, did implement some of their principles, but there were difficulties in applying these, particularly as the conflict moved toward an end and the prisoners were to be repatriated. Many prisoners held by the United States did not want to return to their homelands, and the problem of prisoner repatriation became one of the biggest stumbling blocks to armistice talks.

The education and information programs for Korean prisoners were seemingly successful. Nevertheless, while many prisoners benefited from the programs, especially literacy, agriculture, and news programs, the overall program contributed to polarization among prisoners, with committed communist prisoners, for example, working to disrupt civic education classes.

The Vietnam War

U.S. forces were not directly responsible for prisoner and detainee operations during the Vietnam War. Rather, they supported programs run by the South Vietnamese. U.S. forces did seek to ensure that these programs followed what they deemed applicable conventions, in part to persuade North Vietnamese forces to treat U.S. prisoners better.

(Although the United States maintained that the hostilities constituted an armed international conflict, the North Vietnamese contended the conflict was an internal one and that the Geneva Conventions were not applicable.)

The Vietnam War was the first in which U.S. forces conducted a motivation and morale survey of prisoners and detainees. This assessment showed that insurgents' military power and resources did not appear to have much effect on their morale. The Viet Cong was grossly outnumbered and outgunned by the United States, yet its morale seemed unshaken. More broadly, the motivation and morale survey demonstrated that understanding what makes U.S. enemies want to continue fighting is crucially important for the conduct of the war, particularly when seeking to determine the resilience of unconventional or asymmetric adversaries.

Iraqi Operations

The military victory of the United States in the major combat operations in the Iraq conflict was quick and decisive, but the post-combat occupation was a more extended operation.

Several factors led to some of the early failures of post-combat operations in Iraq. As the insurgency grew, U.S. forces at first assumed that poverty (economic subsistence) and religious extremism were the primary motivators. They designed battlefield strategies and detainee programs accordingly. Later it was learned that, in many cases, infusions of cash into troubled areas merely provided an additional source of income for opportunistic, not impoverished, criminals or insurgents. These assumptions could have been tested by surveying detainees, but this capacity did not exist early on.

In addition, there was a shortage of trained personnel to carry out detainee operations, official doctrine was out of step with the realities of the conflict in Iraq, and there was a reluctant realization that a growing insurgency would require a different approach to detainee operations.

The prisoner abuse scandal at the Abu Ghraib detention facility in 2004 heightened awareness of detention operations and invigorated efforts to update doctrine, training, and leadership. Changes had to keep pace with the growing insurgency and the surge of U.S. forces, which resulted in a sharp increase in the number of detainees housed in Coalition internment facilities. In 2007, the number of detainees nearly doubled, from about 15,000 to more than 25,000. This prompted commanders to undertake several steps to improve detainee operations, including creating a more-refined classification of the detainee population, instituting educational and vocational programs, and attempting to make the detention and release process more transparent.

Several problems plagued these efforts. Within the military, many soldiers and Marines viscerally questioned the release of some detainees, who, in their view, would begin or continue to fight once released from Coalition custody. Initial detainee classification systems were not completely successful, sufficient funding for detainee operations was not always forthcoming from Washington policymakers, and some reintegration and rehabilitation efforts were based on erroneous assumptions about the detainee population, including its religiosity and level of education.

MNF-I commanders realized that detention operations should focus on identifying and separating high-risk detainees (who would eventually be turned over to the Iraqi justice system) from detainees who would inevitably be released and reintegrated into Iraqi society. They also realized that they had an opportunity to turn a strategic risk into a strategic advantage by seeking to understand the motivations and circumstances of the detainee population and by developing a strategic communication campaign aimed at the Iraqi people and the wider regional audience. To both determine how to separate the detainees and to capitalize on this opportunity, in late 2007, U.S. officials initiated a transition-in survey for all new detainees.

Special Populations

Iraq detainee operations also involved several special populations, such as juveniles, women, those convicted by the Iraqi criminal court system, and political refugees. Although juveniles were a small proportion of all detainees in Iraq, their numbers more than tripled in 2007, from less than 300 to more than 900. Juvenile detainees were of mixed social and educational status and were detained for alleged offenses of varying seriousness. Planning for detainee operations, particularly those for asymmetric conflicts, will likely have to address similar unusual populations and characteristics.

Conclusions and Recommendations

Prisoner and detainee operations in recent U.S. military operations have followed a typical pattern: underestimation of the number of prisoners and detainees which would be held, hasty scrambling for resources to meet the operational needs, and doctrine and policy that did not provide the needed guidance, given the operational reality. Historically, the initial phase of capture and subsequent "care-and-custody" of detainees has included improvisation and crisis management, giving way to an eventual but more concerted and erratic effort to improve operations. During the later phases of military operations, an attempt is often made to educate prisoners and detainees and influence their social and political values. There is some evidence that these programs have a positive effect; however, designing these programs without some basic understanding of the detainee population can lead to missteps and wasted effort.

Prior to detention, U.S. forces must plan how to provide for the care and custody of detainees. In almost every conflict, there has been an underestimation of the number of detainees and a delay in expanding detention operations. Going into a major conflict, policymakers and planners should prepare to monitor changes in the size of the detention population and prepare to fund needed expansion of detention facilities. A surge in troops is likely to lead to a surge in detainees.

Initial interactions with detainees should aim to extract time-sensitive information relevant to battlefield operations as well as collection of "atmospherics" that can provide a deeper or broader understanding of the adversary. Collecting this information during the first hours or days of detention, before the detainee has had a chance to interact with others in the detention camp, would provide an unvarnished picture of the enemy and allow analysts to gauge changes in motivation over time. This survey can also provide the initial classification of the detainee, assisting in correct placement of the detainee in camp housing.

Once in detention, a more-thorough survey of detainees can help inform detainee programs and assess the risks detainees pose to each other. Coalition officials also need to develop measures of effectiveness for detainee programs; especially important is tracking recidivism rates for released detainees, as well as the effects of a strategic communication plan on public opinion in the host nation and internationally.

In Iraq, doctrinal shortcomings regarding detainee operations contributed to a climate that may have fed into the Abu Ghraib scandal. Doctrine on detainee operations should provide guidance on the legal requirements of detention; legal issues of who should be detained and for how long have affected operations in Iraq, Vietnam, and Korea. Doctrine should be reviewed and updated to provide guidance on how to establish detainee operations and how to integrate detainee operations within a broader counterinsurgency doctrine.

Acknowledgments

The authors acknowledge three successive commanders of TF-134—MG William Brandenburg (USA), LTG John "Jack" Gardner (USA), LtGen. Doug Stone (USMC), and former MNF-I Commander GEN David Petraeus (USA)—for their time, encouragement, and support and the unprecedented, on-the-ground access they provided to detainee operations in Iraq. We also thank COL Mark Martins, former MNF-I Staff Judge Advocate (USA); COL Wes Martin, former TF-134 J-3 (USA); COL William Ivey, former TF-134 Deputy Commander (USA); and TF-134 Senior Cultural Advisor Steve Jabar. We thank MAJ Jim Stordahl (USA) for being an excellent liaison for our research activities while on the ground in Iraq from 2007 to 2008, and LTC Paul Yingling (USA) for continuing that tradition of late. We thank our RAND colleagues Clifford Grammich and Judy Larson for their sharp and incisive editing of this report, and RAND colleague Jeff Marquis for his review of the Vietnam chapter. Most importantly, we thank our colleagues for their tireless effort on the ground in Iraq from 2007–2008: Austin Long, Kathe Jervis, Tom Fisher, Kayla Williams, and Rebecca BouChebel. We owe a special debt of gratitude to the team's administrative assistant in the United States, Karin Suede, who made the team's deployments to Iraq possible, and to our security liaison, Jordan Bell-Zorich. Finally, we thank our RAND colleague Terry Kelly and Jim Powlen from Logos Technologies for their reviews of this publication. The authors are solely responsible for any errors of fact or opinion.

Abbreviations

BBA	bilingual, bicultural advisor
CCCI	Central Criminal Court of Iraq
CI&E	Command for Information and Education
CJTF-7	Combined Joint Task Force 7
CORDS	Civil Operations and Rural Development Support
CPA	Coalition Provisional Authority
DoD	Department of Defense
GOI	Government of Iraq
ICEX	infrastructure coordination and exploitation
IED	improvised explosive device
IIG	Interim Iraqi Government
MACV	Military Assistance Command, Vietnam
MEK	Mujahedin-e Khalq
MNC-I	Multi-National Corps–Iraq
MNF-I	Multi-National Force–Iraq
NLF	National Liberation Front
OSD	Office of the Secretary of Defense

POW	prisoner of war
TF	Task Force
TIF	Theater Internment Facility
TIFRC	Theater Internment Facility Reconciliation Centers
UN	United Nations
UNSCR	United Nations Security Council Resolution
USIS	United States Information Service

CHAPTER ONE

The Recurring Importance of Prisoner and Detainee Operations

In the course of military actions following the September 11, 2001, terrorist attacks against the United States, detainees and how to manage them have been increasingly controversial topics for U.S., allied, Middle Eastern, and other policymakers and publics. "Guantanamo Bay" and "Abu Ghraib" became provocative shorthand terms for examples of how detainee operations could go wrong if clear and current doctrine did not exist.

In many ways, the problems at Abu Ghraib stemmed from a failure within high-level policy circles in Washington to plan sufficiently for detainee operations—i.e., a failure to anticipate the need to detain large numbers of individuals, to have in place an adequate doctrine for doing so, and to have trained and disciplined personnel to understand and execute the doctrine. Such failures have had serious consequences for U.S. military and diplomatic efforts. The Abu Ghraib scandal put the United States in a defensive posture, causing the focus of its detainee operations to shift toward the basics: training military policemen, guards, intelligence personnel, and soldiers to uphold a higher standard with respect to the treatment of detainees.

From the beginning of the U.S. intervention in Iraq in 2003, policymakers in Washington and Baghdad who were responsible for detention had improvised plans for detainee operations. They had not expected that the surrender terms dictated by the Coalition to conventionally arrayed Iraqi forces would result in the detention and housing of large numbers of enemy combatants or the need for a parole system. They were reluctant to accept the existence of a sizable insurgency and, hence, did not have adequate capacity to manage increasing numbers of detainees. The U.S. Army, which had primary responsibility for combat operations in Iraq, lacked an overall counterinsurgency doctrine. When one was developed, it did not fully include doctrine related to detainee operations. Policymakers also failed to appreciate the importance of a multidisciplinary understanding of the cultural, social, political, and economic motivations of the detainees who were captured during the insurgency.

The problems U.S. forces encountered conducting detainee operations in Iraq stemmed from two principal shortfalls: the lack of appropriate technical competencies and the lack of clear policy and doctrine. These problems were not unique to operations in Iraq. Indeed, the history of major U.S. conflicts dating to World War II reveals a typical pattern, including

- belated recognition that prisoners will be taken in significant numbers and will need to be managed
- hasty scrambling for resources needed for prisoner or detainee operations
- a period of crisis management often accompanied by negative incidents
- a concerted but difficult effort to improve operations
- incipient understanding of the opportunities for influence through reintegration of prisoners into their society
- belated education and integration programs, with outcomes that could have been optimized by better and earlier implementation of a comprehensive plan.

This document synthesizes what is known about prisoner and detainee operations. It includes historical reviews of prisoner and detainee operations since World War II, as well as more-detailed reviews of detainee operations in Iraq and the lessons they offer for doctrine and practice.

In the second chapter, we review efforts to persuade nearly a half-million German prisoners of war (POWs) in U.S. detention facilities of the advantages of democracy over fascism. These efforts were controversial at the time, given widespread beliefs—similar to some current ones about Iraqi insurgents—that Nazi soldiers would resist such education. Instead, camp administrators found that prisoners varied widely in their commitment to the Nazi regime and their openness to other ideas. Many participants in camp education programs contributed significantly to postwar West Germany.

In the third chapter, we review efforts to house and educate prisoners in the Korean War. These efforts occurred at a small number of massive camps, one of which housed more than 150,000 prisoners. Among these prisoners, as in World War II, there was a wide range of beliefs, making it necessary to tailor programs to subsets of prisoners. Later, programs were complicated by the reluctance of some prisoners to return to their homelands.

In the fourth chapter, we review detainee operations during the Vietnam conflict, particularly after the escalation of American military involvement. Like those during the Korean War, these efforts had to address varying levels of commitment to the insurgency by detainees, who ranged from uniformed military personnel openly engaging in military actions to sympathizers or clandestine supporters of the insurgency to defectors who wished to rejoin the side of the South Vietnamese government. Vietnamese detainee operations also included a motivation and morale survey that began to explore the types of information that might be gained from prisoners.

In the fifth chapter, we review detainee operations in Iraq. From the commencement of initial combat operations in Iraq through the Abu Ghraib scandal in 2004, detainee operations were slow to develop. During that period, detainee operations varied by facility and the burgeoning numbers of detainees they housed. Beginning in late 2004, a more-comprehensive attempt was made to uniformly revamp detainee operations across the country, to emphasize links between detainee and tactical operations in the counterinsurgency, and to develop programs for reintegrating detainees into Iraqi society and in anticipation of the transfer of responsibility for detainee operations to the Government of Iraq (GOI).

In the final chapter, we summarize our research and its implications. This includes a summary of technical issues, such as care of detainees, and doctrinal issues, such as the role detainee operations play in prosecution of the conflict (e.g., through information gathered from detainees) or reconstruction afterwards (e.g., through education and rehabilitation of detainees).

Despite the inevitability and ultimate importance of detainee operations in military conflicts, policymakers have repeatedly treated such operations as an afterthought and then struggled to make them more effective. Developing doctrine on what is ultimately an opportunity to be leveraged can improve both military operations and post-conflict reconstruction.

CHAPTER TWO

U.S. Programs for German Prisoners in World War II

World War II, a conventional conflict, and the prisoners taken during it differ from more-recent conflicts and their prisoners or detainees. Yet there are parallels between prisoner operations in World War II and those of subsequent conflicts.

More specifically, three initial misjudgments in handling German prisoners have recurred over time. While eventually corrected in World War II, they adversely affected U.S. interests and detainee operations both then and in subsequent conflicts.

- Military planners underestimated the number of prisoners the Allies would take and the speed at which they would take them. It is difficult to explain this oversight, given the scale of World War II.
- U.S. military authorities viewed German prisoners as a homogeneous grouping of Nazis. Not until serious problems, stemming from ideological differences, erupted among the prisoners did authorities realize that there were subgroups that were hostile to each other and whose political values and attitudes toward the conflict and their captors were very different.
- U.S. policymakers were slow to realize that prisoners should not simply be warehoused and used to fill labor needs but that their internment provided an opportunity to help shape both the continuing conflict and postwar Europe. This overlooked a basic dynamic. Within prison camps, rival parties sought to recruit

new followers, hardliners guarded against any softening of ideological positions, and members of opposing factions fought each other, sometimes to the death. At the same time, by having been removed from combat, captured individuals had a greater chance to survive the conflict and thereby presented an opportunity to shape their post-conflict society. World War II was almost over before U.S. policymakers had these insights.

Arrival and Administration

Shortly after its entry into World War II, the U.S. government established the Office of the Provost Marshal General. Among other duties, this office was to have responsibility for the custody of interned civilians and POWs. There was little initial indication how large POW operations would be. By May 1942, the United States had only 32 POWs, mostly resulting from sinking of U-boats off the coast of North Carolina (Billinger, 2000).[1]

Soon the North African campaign and, later, the European campaign would bring in large waves of German prisoners. In some cases, the speed of surrender overtook the ability of Allied forces to oversee it, resulting in long lines "of captured Afrika Korps soldiers marching toward a POW processing center, unguided and unguarded" (Krammer, 1979, p. 3).

Increasingly, the ships and trucks that moved U.S. troops to the front were used on their return journey to move POWs to the United States. Eventually, more than 400,000 German POWs were held in more than 500 facilities across the United States, with camps located in all but three states.

Initial activities for prisoners included using the enlisted men among them as workers, principally in farming and logging, to overcome wartime labor shortages and as permitted by international con-

---

[1]   The United States also interned several thousand U.S. citizens of Japanese, German, and Italian ancestry.

ventions.[2] The location of camps followed local labor needs. Employers paid the government for this labor, helping to defray the costs of running the camps.

Still, lack of preparation for a POW influx caused a number of administrative problems, many of which were to recur in subsequent conflicts. The German language posed some difficulties for interrogators and administrators, particularly given persistent shortages of translators and an even greater dearth of clerks, typists, guards, and administrators with German language skills. One camp with about 10,000 prisoners could claim only one staff member fluent in German (Krammer, 1979). Similar language difficulties would recur in later conflicts. Incorrect recording of unfamiliar names (and inconsistencies transcribing German characters, such as *ü, ä, ö,* and *ß*) led to confusion about the identities of prisoners and allowed some high-value prisoners to escape notice. Even some ordinary prisoners deliberately confused records and identities as a minor act of sabotage or to give themselves a "promotion" that would translate into better living conditions.

The inability of camp administrators to communicate properly with their prisoners perhaps contributed to their view of the prisoners as a monolithic group. Initially, nobody investigated whether there were internal divisions or ideological distinctions among the prisoners that should be noted for administrative purposes and perhaps be used for strategic advantage.

This made it possible for Nazi leadership to reassert itself among the prisoners, sometimes even by the time they reached the United States (Koop, 1988). The reassertion of Nazi leadership did not initially disturb the American captors because it resulted in a disciplined, self-policing prisoner population. When problems arose, American authorities initially associated anti-Nazi prisoners with the disorder, not realizing that in many instances they represented pro-democratic voices trying to resist the internal Nazi leadership of their camp (Koop, 1988).

---

[2] Article 27 of the Geneva Convention of 1929 exempted officers from such mandatory labor but allowed it for enlisted ranks. Noncommissioned officers could be given supervisory roles or paid to conduct regular labor. Officers could be given work upon their request. Article 31 prohibits making prisoners perform work with a "direct connection with the operations of the war" (Geneva Convention Relative to the Treatment of Prisoners of War, 1929).

Committed Nazis were thus able to intimidate and control their fellow prisoners. They set up a censorship program to review incoming newspapers and remove any articles unfavorable to Germany, shielding their fellow prisoners from facts about the unfolding war. In some instances they infiltrated the mail room and spied on the private correspondence of the other prisoners to determine their political sentiments. They displayed portraits of Adolf Hitler and required testimonials of allegiance. They beat and even killed many open dissidents as well as those whose loyalty they questioned (Koop, 1988).

At first, U.S. camp administrators sought to protect what they perceived to be a vulnerable minority of anti-Nazi prisoners. Because few prisoners were openly willing to identify themselves as anti-Nazi, the initial anti-Nazi groups became a collection of obvious outsiders of all sorts, including an entire division of political dissidents (Communists and Social Democrats) and criminals who had been sent against their will to fight and had surrendered at the first opportunity.

Delays in Disaggregating the Prisoner Population

Belatedly, as U.S. camp administrators began to direct their attention to the ideological and political divisions among the prisoners, they realized that it was actually the committed Nazis who were in the minority and ought to be segregated. American journalists also began to investigate the issue of Nazi control of prisoner populations in the United States. Their critical reports were instrumental in prodding U.S. camp administrators to assess the diversity of views among prisoners.[3]

The prisoners were, of course, soldiers in Hitler's military, and some were Nazi Party members. Many continued to sympathize with some aspects of National Socialism, to admire Hitler, or to adhere to German nationalism. Yet the bulk of prisoners were not hardliners.

Among the Allies, the United States had lagged in realizing the need to understand the composition of the prisoner population and to

---

[3]   E.g., Bromley, 1944. For more on research to understand the mindsets of German prisoners, see, among others, Ansbacher, 1948; Shils and Janowitz, 1948; and Peak, 1945.

design policies recognizing differences among the prisoners. Initially, the only separation was of enemy officers from enlisted men, as international protocols required.

The British took a more-calibrated approach from the start. They initially categorized prisoners who were committed Nazis as "black," those who did not show a strong ideological commitment as "grey," and those who were committed anti-Nazis as "white" (Krammer, 1979). Later, the "black" category was split into "ardent Nazis" and "Nazis," and the "grey" category was split into "dark grey" and "light grey."

It is difficult to determine the consequences of the U.S. failure to classify and segregate prisoners sooner. As might be expected, the segregation of Nazi hardliners stopped the murders, beatings, and intimidation among prisoners. Yet the failure to initially segregate the prisoners may have also had more longstanding consequences. One historian writes, "Although a program was later initiated to 'democratize' the . . . prisoners . . . the best opportunity to segregate the[m by] ideology had passed, and totalitarian reinforcement" took place (Krammer, 1979, p. 14).

Nevertheless, while we cannot conclude that the bullying and intimidation had only temporary effects to reinforce Nazi ideology, there is solid evidence that even the belated democratization program had some positive effects.

Reeducation Programs

Among the Allies, the Soviets were the first to attempt to reeducate POWs, launching their program in October 1941, two months before the United States entered the war. German Communist émigrés led the effort. Their first approach was to appeal to the "common man" among the prisoners. Initially the program had little success. Among the causes for program difficulties may have been that, first, the war was still going well for Germany at that time, and, second, influence in the regimented German army flowed hierarchically, necessitating the inclusion of officers in any conversion effort (Krammer, 1979).

The Soviets eventually identified an older, anti-Nazi officer who was also a veteran of World War I. He began to "proselytize" among his fellow officers, making little headway until the German military catastrophe at Stalingrad. In one of his subsequent speeches, he "urged his listeners to remain loyal to the people of Germany but to reject the criminal acts that were being perpetrated in their name by the Nazis" (Smith, 1996, p. 7). This was not quite the message that the Soviets, who wished to develop communist leadership for postwar Germany, had in mind. Yet his words resonated strongly. Seeing this, the Soviets quickly printed and distributed a half-million copies of the speech. After Stalingrad, the Soviets were also able to persuade several other German officers to renounce their allegiance to Hitler and call on their soldiers to surrender. Their numbers eventually included more than fifty generals, the prize among them being Field Marshall Friedrich Paulus, who had commanded the German forces at Stalingrad.

The defection of the officers and growing recognition that Germany would lose the war increased the willingness of the prisoners to participate in the *Antifa*, or Antifascism, classes. The schools set up to teach this program sought to inculcate values of antimilitarism and antifascism and to indoctrinate participants to communism. Graduates had to pledge that they would fight militarism and fascism. They were then deployed as recruiters in the camps or assigned to work with the Soviet military on psychological operations (Smith, 1996).

Perhaps the key difference between the treatment of prisoners by the Soviets and that by the other Allies was in the forthright intent of the Soviets to develop a cadre of postwar leaders (Smith, 1996). Walter Ulbricht, the first leader of East Germany, was a graduate of the program, as were many of his leading officials.

The United States was reluctant to push a comparable reeducation program among its own German prisoners for fear that it would violate international protocol and lead to retaliatory measures against U.S. prisoners held by Germany. While many German expatriates in the United States pressed for a pro-democracy initiative among the prisoners, they, unlike German expatriates in the Soviet Union, did not have political ambitions for postwar Germany.

An even larger obstacle to a U.S. program, one with parallels in subsequent conflicts, was the assumption that the prisoners were hardened ideologues. They were widely assumed to be inclined toward fascism because of the German "national character," the after-effects of recent political humiliations, or even a cultural inclination to the authoritarian or the grandiose. Some believed that a sound defeat and the elimination of Nazi leadership would take care of German military aggression better than any well-intentioned pedagogy.

Nevertheless, U.S. proponents of a reeducation project eventually prevailed. This occurred as camp administrators realized that most prisoners were not committed ideologues, U.S. policymakers wished to compete with the Soviet program, awareness increased that it would be unwise to return prisoners with totalitarian inclinations to a postwar Germany, and pressure arose from the American media and a small but persistent group of experts for reeducation.

The initial prisoner education efforts did not have a clear focus but, rather, consisted of several strands. Classes offered factual information about the United States, democracy, and the conduct of the war, including German atrocities and crimes against humanity. Instructors also encouraged prisoners to read literature. Camp administrators facilitated the establishment of camp newspapers and radio programs as an exercise in liberal democracy.

The reeducation program overlaid "social offerings" already in place for prisoners.[4] All camps had initially instituted leisure programs, including movie nights, sport events, amateur theatre, arts and crafts studios, music classes, language instruction, and lectures on local flora and fauna and state history. In many camps, prisoners were encouraged to set up their own internal education programs, with teachers, craftsmen, and professionals among them offering classes in subjects such as shorthand, chemistry, and carpentry. Prisoners were also able to enroll in correspondence courses at more than one hundred American colleges and universities. Many used such education to rise to prominence

---

[4]   Such offerings reflected the concerns of Article 17 of the 1929 Geneva Convention, which stated that "belligerents shall encourage as much as possible the organization of intellectual and sporting pursuits by the prisoners of war" (Geneva Convention, 1929).

after the war, including Ruediger von Wechmar, who became bureau chief of the United Press in Bonn, and Walter Horst Littman, who became senior chemist in the West German Department of Defense (Krammer, 1979).

These initial offerings sought to prevent boredom, and resulting disciplinary problems, among prisoners. The reeducation program had broader goals, albeit contested. Some, arguing that "global warfare requires global thinking," wanted the program to counter acceptance of authoritarianism among the prisoners by inculcating critical thinking skills (Robin, 1995, p. 54). Others saw the defusing of German nationalism as the principal goal of reeducation.[5]

A unique feature of the program was that it was largely kept secret. For reasons that are not fully clear, the existence of the program was not made public until after the war, despite growing press criticism about the assumed absence of such a program.

The Provost Marshal General created a Special Project Division to oversee the program. A group of scholars, émigrés, and cooperating prisoners, which eventually became known as the Idea Factory, oversaw the program.[6] The émigrés carefully screened program participants—who, as a result, strongly resembled the profile of their screeners—favoring disaffected former leftists, intellectuals, and writers.[7] Subgroups were responsible for reviewing film materials, evaluating suggested reading matter, translating recommended materials, monitoring the contents of the growing number of camp newspapers, and producing a central

---

[5]   One proponent of this view was Henry Ehrmann, a German exile who had briefly been interned in a concentration camp before escaping to the United States and gaining work at the New School for Social Research (Robin, 1995). He played a key role in development of the reeducation program, asserting his belief that aggressive militaristic nationalism needed to be transformed into apolitical cultural nationalism, or what might more properly be called patriotism.

[6]   At the high point, 85 prisoners helped to produce newspaper articles and radio scripts as well as to translate curriculum materials for the program.

[7]   For example, to select participants for one program, the émigrés and their cooperating colleagues in the Idea Factory asked prisoners about the ideas that the German philosopher Fichte expounded, important reforms of the Weimar Republic schools, and characters from the Magic Flute (Krammer, 1979). Such questions were better suited for ascertaining class membership and level of education than for measuring values and attitudes.

newspaper, *Der Ruf* (*The Call*). The group responsible for the overall program also considered issues of effective messaging, developing recommendations on how best to counter Nazi propaganda.

Altogether, the activities of the Special Project Division fell into three categories. The first was countering Nazi thinking among prisoners through print and radio programs. This portion was dramatically expanded after the Allied victory and just before repatriation. The second was an effort to train a group of prisoners to help support U.S. occupation forces after the war as pro-democracy administrators. The third was an intensive democratic reeducation program intended to reach as many prisoners as possible before repatriation.

The effort to train future administrators opened in May 1945 as the Experimental Administrative School for Selected German Prisoners of War. Camp administrators initially identified 17,000 prisoners who had been deemed cooperative and reliable for inclusion in the program, ultimately selecting 3,700 for participation. The program featured sixty-day "semesters." The curriculum included English language, U.S. history, German history, military law, and specialized technical training in administrative skills.

The program sought to portray Germany positively rather than to focus on the evils of Nazism. Its German history courses emphasized those portions of the past that could be interpreted as hospitable to democracy, while its U.S. history courses emphasized the obstacles America faced (such as the Civil War) on its journey to become a fully realized democracy.

An additional program in the period before repatriation gave approximately 25,000 prisoners a six-day "crash course" on democracy (Robin, 1995). This course, which included such topics as "democratic traditions in Germany" and "democratic trends in the world today," also stressed that democratic values were compatible with and even inherent in German culture and history and merely needed to be developed further. Participants were broadly representative of the prisoner population, typically having an elementary-school education and previous employment in a trade or agriculture (Smith, 1996). Program leaders hoped graduates would be able to serve in the police force of occupied Germany.

The Special Program Division showed war crime documentaries and broadcast political radio programs to the remaining prisoners as part of their out-processing. The Special Program Division also took control over all camp newspapers. Previously, the camp newspapers had been semi-independent outlets for the creativity and even the political venting of the prisoners, but, in the period before repatriation, these papers were made into additional platforms for official messages on war crimes and politics.

Unfortunately, there were few formal evaluations of these programs. Furthermore, due to poor interagency coordination, no mechanism was put in place to link the returning graduates with the occupying forces, and thus the programs were not employed as intended upon repatriation. Nevertheless, the programs do not appear to have been in vain. Follow-up interviews in later years found that graduates of the Administrative School had gravitated to jobs in journalism or public affairs, with some, such as Walter Hallstein, who became rector of Frankfurt University and president of the European Economic Forum, achieving considerable prominence (Krammer, 1979). A small survey of 78 graduates found that, two years after repatriation, nearly 25 percent were members of a political party (compared to only 5 percent of the overall population), 64 percent were working for the government, and 40 percent felt that their graduation certificate had been useful to them (Krammer, 1979).

Another survey of 22,000 prisoners polled just before embarkation also found some evidence of declining authoritarian attitudes.[8] A majority of respondents declared that they would be unwilling to fight the same war again, even if German victory were to be assured, although younger prisoners were more willing to consider a return to combat than older ones. A very strong majority was positively inclined toward democracy and willing to try it in Germany, and 74 percent expressed positive feelings toward the United States and Americans (Krammer, 1979). Nevertheless, some pernicious attitudes remained

---

[8]   The prisoners were surveyed after learning that, rather than being sent home, they were to go to France for an additional period of forced labor. Researchers surmised that the effect this had on the spirits of the prisoners likely improved their candor in the survey.

strong among the prisoners. Despite the very graphic documentaries and other visual materials about Nazi atrocities that the prisoners had been forced to view, 70 percent asserted that the Holocaust and other atrocities committed by Hitler's regime were propagandistic fabrications and had not really occurred.

Conclusions

The experience with German prisoners in World War II was the first in the past several decades to suggest the necessity of planning for a large, sudden influx of prisoners before the conflict. The readiness plan should include methods for processing, registering, sorting, segregating, accommodating, overseeing, evaluating, influencing, and releasing the prisoners.

The German prisoner experience was also the first of several to demonstrate that prisoners or detainees may vary widely in their politics, with perhaps only a minority of stalwart ideological supporters of their leadership. British and U.S. findings indicated that roughly 10 percent of the prisoners were firmly committed to Nazism, 10 percent were clearly opposed to it, and the remainder were best described as apolitical or vaguely patriotic.

Recognizing likely ideological diversity among prisoners and segregating them, particularly extremist ones, accordingly can help reduce problems that would otherwise occur in camps and reduce the levels of ideological conflict. Identifying and segregating extremists may not be difficult. Many will likely be proud of their ideology and freely admit to it, while available intelligence and observation of their conduct in detention can help identify others.

Political distinctions among prisoners likewise suggest variations in their receptiveness to new ideas and influences. Some prisoners will have strongly held views that are difficult to change. Others may be loosely attached to dominant beliefs but amenable to influence. Some may have succumbed to false information and be dissuadable by exposure to facts. Some may be opportunists who will follow whatever ideology offers material advantage. Some may be indifferent. Regardless, there is likely to be a significant number that can be influenced with varying levels of nonthreatening persuasion. Key elements in influencing prisoners to change their beliefs can include changes in their perception of the enemy resulting from fair treatment as prisoners, learning that important aspects of one's beliefs are incorrect or were manipulated, acceptance of defeat and the subsequent need to move forward, and discovering the feasibility of new beliefs.

The Idea Factory realized these key elements to varying degrees and lived up to its name through a number of creative approaches. Its principal weakness lay in the arbitrary nature of the group's composition. For example, the strong reliance on émigrés led to the disproportionate selection of intellectuals among the prisoners for extended programs. Émigrés, exiles, and expatriates who help design such programs may also have their own biases and agendas, which policymakers need to carefully consider. The Soviet reeducation programs took explicit advantage of these in developing postwar German leaders among prisoners. The less-specific U.S. programs may have contributed to a pro-democratic West Germany not through pro-democratic offerings but through collateral influences, including the glimpse they gave to prisoners of the cultural freedom and financial prosperity associated with American life.

CHAPTER THREE

Korean War Prisoner Programs

The Korean War began when North Korean forces crossed the 38th parallel and attacked South Korea in late June 1950. Given that the sudden start of the war caught the United States by surprise, the need for handling large numbers of prisoners from the conflict was unanticipated. Sudden, dramatic shifts in the course of the war further complicated the challenge of handling prisoners.

The United States had few resources on site for handling Korean War prisoners. Even though the U.S. and Allied forces had designed, built, and implemented successful prisoner camps and reeducation programs less than a decade earlier for World War II, the lessons learned from managing prisoners in the earlier conflict were not immediately transferred to the Korean War. The U.S. Army had quickly demobilized after World War II, and experienced soldiers had returned to civilian life. As a result, the U.S. Army and the United Nations Command faced many challenges in managing prisoners, including

- lack of qualified personnel, such as interrogators, linguists, and guards
- dependence on even less qualified South Korean guards
- lack of pre-conflict planning for handling massive numbers of prisoners
- lack of cultural, sociological, political, and economic understanding of enemy prisoners
- inability to correctly identify prisoners as communists, anticommunists, civilians, or insurgents

- failure to see influence of prisoners as part of the battle and political process
- difficulty of applying the principles of the new 1949 Geneva Conventions for handling prisoners and civilians to a war of uncertain status, particularly to prisoners who did not wish to be repatriated.

Some of these challenges were easily managed. Others were more difficult and contributed to initial problems within the camps, particularly a lack of security and the lack of a comprehensive understanding of the prisoners. The focus of U.S. forces in prisoner administration wavered from a narrow one of seeking to secure the prisoner population to a broader one of seeking to better understand and work with it toward specific goals.

The goals of prisoner administration also shifted with the different phases of the conflict. The most successful phase for prisoner education was from June 1951 through May 1952. The phase from May 1952 to June 1953 saw increasing problems in controlling prisoners, particularly as armistice talks unfolded. The final phase through December 1953 focused on repatriation questions, which were eventually postponed by transferring prisoners who were reluctant to be repatriated to the Indian Army.

Establishment of Prisoner Camps in Korea

Shortly after the Korean War began, the U.S. Army identified Pusan as a site for housing POWs. By August 1950, Pusan held 1,899 prisoners. U.S. personnel handled all processing and camp operations using South Korean guards. The United States had just signed the 1949 Geneva Conventions, but the Senate had not yet ratified them. Indeed, the State Department requested that Senate consideration be postponed until after the Korean War ended (U.S. Senate Committee on Foreign Relations, 1955). All parties involved in the Korean War signed the Geneva Conventions, but none had ratified them within their domestic law. Accordingly, the Geneva Conventions did not apply to the Korean

War as a matter of law. Nevertheless, all parties pledged to abide by the conventions' principles (Pictet, 1960).[1]

The number of prisoners grew rapidly following the September 1950 landing of a U.S. force at Inch'on that pushed into North Korea. As a result of this maneuver, an estimated 600,000 North Koreans were trapped in South Korea. Most took off their uniforms and melted into the South Korean countryside. Many who disguised themselves as farmers conducted surprise attacks on U.S. and South Korean forces (White, 1957). Because U.S. forces could not distinguish such attackers from civilians, they rounded up a large number of civilians among the military prisoners they took.

By October, there were 62,500 prisoners in Pusan and an additional 33,000 at a new camp hastily built in Inch'on. Additional transit camps were established in the north, and the Army began looking for more space at Pusan to house an additional 100,000 prisoners.

The International Committee of the Red Cross inspected and reported on U.S. treatment of prisoners in Korea. Overall, the Red Cross reported that U.S. treatment of prisoners was "extremely good," especially during the first two years of the war (White, 1957, p. 25). As the Geneva Conventions dictated, the United States provided the same care to the prisoners as it provided to its own soldiers, resulting in better nutrition, health care, and education than most of the prisoners had ever received. Yet the Red Cross did note that prisoners in U.S. camps were denied their right to correspond with their families or to receive parcels (Pictet, 1960). The Red Cross did not have access to prison camps in North Korea.

The December 1950 intervention of Chinese troops on behalf of North Korea forced the U.S. Army to evacuate prisoners from the northern transit camps and transfer them quickly to Pusan. As a result, the number of prisoners in the Pusan camps grew to 137,000. The Army then identified the island of Koje-do as a suitable site for a prison camp. It began building a camp to hold 38,400 prisoners, but the size of the camp reached 153,000 by June 1951. By late summer 1951, Pusan and Koje-do held 163,569 prisoners. Despite the large

---

[1] China did not so pledge until 1952.

number, the Red Cross found that the camps had "reached almost the maximum state of perfection in layout, decorations, and cleanliness" (White, 1957, p. 136).

During the early part of the war, U.S. forces, in accordance with the Third Geneva Convention, separated prisoners only by rank, sex, and nationality. This meant there was no attempt to separate communists and noncommunists. It also meant that soldiers and civilians were mixed together, in violation of the Fourth Geneva Convention (Article 84). As interrogators worked with arriving prisoners, they found a large number who wished to join the fight against North Korea. Many of these were South Koreans or Chinese Nationalists and were either civilians mistakenly taken prisoner or soldiers pressed into service by the North Korean or Chinese armies. The Geneva Conventions forbid compelling POWs or interned civilians to fight against their own forces. The United States interpreted this requirement to forbid allowing prisoners to volunteer to join the fight against the communists. This led to resentment among some prisoners, who now considered themselves political prisoners rather than POWs.

Initial Education Programs

Education programs for the prisoners originated with a U.S. Army pilot project in October 1950 at Yongdong-po, near Seoul, for 500 prisoners, primarily comprising farmers, laborers, clerks, merchants, and teachers. These "political education" classes, very similar to the education programs for German prisoners held by the United States in World War II, included Army news releases and commentaries, weekly United States Information Service (USIS) translations and news releases, and films that had been used in Japan to explain democracy. The pilot program also included voluntary Christian church services as well as visits from South Korean officials and businessmen who explained to the prisoners their ideas for building democracy in Korea (White, 1957). Before the Army could assess the benefits of the pilot program, the Chinese joined the fight, and the program was transferred to the United Nations (UN) Command.

When Koje-do opened early in 1951, administrators developed an education plan to teach skills needed in the camp—and some others as well. These included carpentry, masonry, tailoring, shoe repair, machining, electric utility work, painting, motor maintenance, and boat repair. The objectives of the plan were threefold: to provide beneficial occupations for interested prisoners, to offer prisoners an opportunity to acquire semitechnical skills, and to establish sources of production for badly needed items. The UN Command, however, was less interested in the educational benefit of the plan and approved only the third objective, to produce items needed by the camps, which required using only prisoners with existing skills (U.S. Army Pacific Headquarters, 1960). The upshot of this approach was that only skilled prisoners were included in the prison programs, which had little if any educational value, and the vast majority of the camp population, numbering more than 100,000, was left idle.

Camp administrators changed their approach in March 1951 when the USIS conducted its first large-scale program in the camps, giving one news sheet (translated into Korean and Chinese) to each tent group of 62 prisoners. A subsequent survey found 50,000 prisoners read the news sheet. Camp administrators quickly doubled production of the news sheet as a way to reach the "hearts and minds" of the former combatants (U.S. Army Pacific Headquarters, 1960).

A secondary result of this information campaign was a significant increase of interest in literacy programs, and voluntary reading and literacy groups rose among the prisoners. Camp administrators also found that the news sheet helped reduce fear of the United States among prisoners.

These results prodded the UN Command to seek a prisoner education program that would provide "an understanding and appreciation of the political, social, and economic objectives and activities of the United Nations and to assist them in . . . becom[ing] better citizens in their country" (U.S. Army Pacific Headquarters, 1960, p. 104). The UN Command therefore established in April 1951 a Command for Information and Education (CI&E) to "initiate, organize, and operate an orientation and education program for North Korean and Chinese communist prisoners of war" (U.S. Army Pacific Headquarters, 1960,

p. 105). The program began in June 1951 at Koje-do and included the vocational training that the U.S. Army had suggested when Koje-do first opened.

In one compound of 7,500 Korean prisoners, the educational program began with the political education program that the U.S. Army had pioneered and additional classes in carpentry. The program expanded rapidly to include eleven activities involving at least 130,000 prisoners and detainees. Table 3.1 lists and briefly describes these activities (U.S. Army Pacific Headquarters, 1960, p. 106).

Each participating compound had a CI&E office, an instructional center, classrooms, a library, reading rooms, and a movie projector and screen. These centers usually housed the orientation classes, dramas and concerts, films, health classes, and library activities. Radio broadcasts were handled at a central location, while group meetings, literacy school, and agriculture classes were generally held in prisoners' quarters.

The factual news reporting of the education program, including USIS political education broadcasts, newsreels, and a current events magazine, proved critical in explaining UN and democratic aims. While not all prisoners attended educational programs featuring these materials, the USIS broadcasts reached everyone in the camps and made it more difficult for Communist Party operatives to conduct propaganda campaigns among the prisoners.

The literacy training became one of the most important benefits of the education program. During the Japanese occupation of World War II, Koreans had been taught only Japanese in school, leaving most illiterate in their native language. Many Chinese prisoners were also illiterate.

The agricultural training had both immediate and long-term benefits. Koje-do had about 30 acres of arable land available within the camp and 300 acres of steep hillside outside it. The agricultural training program included clearing and dividing the land into plots for clover and barley production. American experts helped prisoners experiment with various fertilizers to treat the soil. They showed that the fertilizers were twice as effective as the human feces the Korean farmers had traditionally used for fertilizer and also less likely to spread disease

Table 3.1
Initial Basic Education Program for Korean and Chinese Prisoners of War

Activity	Description
Orientation	All prisoners were required to have four hours weekly on democracy and the aims of the United Nations. This later became voluntary when communists tried to keep others from going to the programs.
Radio broadcasting	Supported education activities but also included live broadcasts from within compounds and rebroadcasts of the Korean Broadcast System; emphasis on instruction, entertainment, and news
Vocational training	Helped compounds to be self-sufficient; developed skills in carpentry, blacksmithing, shoe repair, straw weaving, tailoring, bricklaying, and barbering
Agricultural training	Considered most valuable, given that most prisoners were farmers; included classroom instruction, demonstrations, and practical applications
Literacy training	Reading taught to those not having fourth-grade equivalent skills; more helpful with Koreans than Chinese, who were hostile to Korean instructors
School continuance	For prisoners under 19 years of age whose education had been interrupted by military service; included language, history, geography, physics, chemistry, and mathematics
Library	Included current periodicals and more than 10,000 volumes on fiction, as well as world and homeland affairs
Athletics	Each prisoner had four hours of calisthenics per week. Open areas were also used for sports.
Recreation	Music, drama, and movies were popular offerings. Drawing, art, woodcarving, sculpturing, choral and instrumental concerts, folk dancing exhibitions, and music classes were also provided.
Youth organizations	Boy Scout troops, which had been popular in Korea before the war, were organized
Health education	Basic personal hygiene and camp sanitation to help prevent disease

(White, 1957). In March 1952, more than 22,000 students enrolled in agriculture classes on Koje-do and other camps. These classes produced cabbage for kimchi, the Korean national dish, and many other vegetables that helped reduce scurvy (U.S. Army Pacific Headquarters, 1960).

Prisoner labor helped supplement some of the education programs and other elements of camp administration. Skilled workers installed stoves and lighting and did plumbing and sewage system work. Prisoners also made bricks and metal roofing and performed all camp housekeeping duties, including cooking (U.S. Army Pacific Headquarters, 1960). Prisoners also helped the Army interview other prisoners, reviewed leaflets for psychological operations, and helped in writing and translation. About 2,500 prisoners served on the CI&E staff by teaching, leading drama groups, and assisting a vocational training program. Prisoners with medical training worked in the camp hospital, and the U.S. Army offered medical training programs to increase the numbers of medical assistants and nurses so as to relieve demands on U.S. doctors working there. Outside the camps, prison labor helped build dams and roads and, by December 1951, helped to manufacture items such as mattresses, comforters, and rice bags needed for civil relief.

The CI&E program caused tensions between camp administrators, who only wanted skilled prisoners to produce goods for the camp, and CI&E program officers, who wanted to develop the indigenous skills of less-skilled Koreans. One reason for this tension was that skilled craftsmen were needed both to build things for the camp and to serve as instructors in the educational program. Ultimately, a compromise allowed about half of the skilled craftsmen to operate shops and teach other prisoners skills to make things for the camp (U.S. Army Pacific Headquarters, 1960).

Broader tensions over the program proved more difficult to resolve. U.S. camp commanders had varied reactions to the program. One considered it a violation of the spirit of the Geneva Conventions and "ordered it discontinued," another "supported it to the extent that it furnished his camp," and a third "threatened to court-martial CI&E representatives," with the net result being that all three failed to realize the "potential value" of the program and its "effect on prisoners' minds" (White, 1957, p. 112).

The Geneva Conventions stipulated that participation in educational programs be voluntary, lest the programs be vehicles for propaganda (Pictet, 1960). Many camp commanders followed the conventions to the letter and interpreted the education program, especially the political orientation activities, as a possible violation of the conventions, despite a Red Cross finding that the program (as it became more established) was indeed purely voluntary (White, 1957). The resulting freedom of choice given to prisoners allowed hard-core communists to avoid the political training on democracy while using the vocational training and materials production classes to make weapons.

Yet the hard-core communists were a small minority of the prison population, and most prisoners participated in the CI&E projects with varying effects. Most were, in fact, eager to learn all they could about the West and the United States. One administrator noted that nothing "worked faster than his distribution of Montgomery Ward and Sears Roebuck catalogues" to show how Americans lived and to counter communist contentions about life in the United States (White, 1957, p. 115). The catalogues also provided inspiration to prison artisans, who became adept at copying items.

Polarization Among Prisoners

As noted earlier, camp administrators differentiated prisoners only by their rank, sex, and nationality. Even identifying prisoners by rank and nationality proved to be difficult, given the desperate shortage of Korean and Chinese linguists. The inability of interrogators and camp administrators to distinguish between hard-core and less-committed communists, noncommunists, hard-core anticommunists, civilians, and insurgents eventually affected camp operations adversely.

The U.S. Army was desperately short not only of Chinese and Korean linguists but also of trained guards, forcing it to rely on poorly trained South Korean guards. U.S. draftees were also quite young; most lacked the experience of soldiers who had been in World War II and had received inadequate training. The number of guards was also insufficient; Koje-do was estimated to have less than one-fifth of the guards it needed (Gebhardt, 2005).

At first, camp commanders were indifferent to violence between communists and anticommunists, reasoning that their obligations were those of the Geneva Conventions requiring them to clothe and feed the prisoners. (This was, of course, in violation of the Third and Fourth Conventions' requirement that prisoners be protected from all acts of violence and intimidation.) As the violence escalated, commanders became less sure how to uphold Article 121 of the Third Convention, placing responsibility for the death or injury of any prisoner, even if caused by another prisoner, with the holding power, while also upholding Article 16, requiring the holding power to treat all prisoners alike, regardless of race, nationality, religious belief, or political opinion. One administrator noted:

> Read together, the two articles meant that if we failed to segregate, we would be responsible for the deaths, but each faction must get equal treatment. We now went about the delicate task of pulling them apart. . . . As for us—the American captors— few then realized that we soon were to have the painful task of umpiring an important part of Korea's Civil War, which, revived by our good food, was to rise in our POW camps. It was, for the moment, our duty only to put a stop to those mangled corpses which appeared at the compound gates, before the neutral Swiss could protest. Let these North Koreans fight it out after they got back home, we said. It had thus far occurred to no one that some might even refuse to return. (White, 1957, p. 82)

Once administrators segregated communist and noncommunist prisoners by compound, exposure to the CI&E program began to vary. The two hard-core communist compounds were able to greatly reduce their exposure to the CI&E program, while communist operatives in the more lax, mixed compounds were able to terrorize, intimidate, and prevent less-fervent believers from participating. The result was a polarization of the two sides and an increase in violence. Seemingly universal activities, such as the Boy Scouts, which had been popular in Korea and China before the war, were now rent by more militant groups, such as the Komsomol Youth Brigades on the communist side or the Korean Young Men's Anti-Communist League on the other (White, 1957). Polarization and violence increased as each faction struggled for control of the camps. The first uprising occurred in June 1951, just as the CI&E program was launched, and was followed by many more, not just at Koje-do but in all the prison camps. Soon UN Command personnel were unable to enter some compounds at night.

The loss of command meant that camp commanders could not perform their judicial duties. They were not able to collect evidence or find witnesses who would testify. The UN Command had also prohibited trials while armistice talks, which began in July 1951, were ongoing. As a result, for much of the summer and fall of 1951 the UN Command worked to regain control of the camps but had few levers to do so.

The disintegration of order in the camps quickly became a central concern for U.S. Army and UN leadership. By December 1951, more than 9,000 U.S. and South Korean personnel were stationed on Koje-do, but administrators wanted 6,000 more. Riots, assaults, and murder continued within the camps. In February 1952, a battalion-sized force failed to dislodge the communist leadership of one compound of 9,000 prisoners on Koje-do (Gebhardt, 2005). The height of camp disorder at Koje-do occurred when the camp commander was taken hostage in May 1952 and released three days later after the UN Command acceded to prisoner demands, including those to halt the screening of prisoners (Gebhardt, 2005; Hermes, 1988). At this point, it appeared that the camps had been infiltrated to a large extent by communist operatives, and the prisoners were receiving instructions from the North Korean military in an effort to influence the armistice negotiations. These disturbances were a pointed reminder of the often fatal consequences of a lack of a comprehensive, deep understanding of prisoner and detainee populations.

The U.S. Army was able to reestablish effective control over Koje-do in June 1952, but only after a three-hour battle that cost the lives of 31 prisoners and one U.S. soldier (White, 1957). Following this incident, the UN Command initiated Operation SCATTER, which also screened prisoners for repatriation.

Occasional problems still flared. For example, in the summer of 1952, camp administrators issued each prisoner a summer uniform of bright red. This delighted the Chinese communists but angered the Koreans, both communist and noncommunist, who remembered the red uniforms Japanese occupiers of World War II had issued to prisoners. This unfortunate incident occurred just before the anniversary of the defeat of Japan, marking the independence of both North and South Korea and a national holiday in both. In the resulting riots, prisoners threw out their clothes and pelted South Korean guards with rocks, who in turn opened fire and killed several prisoners (White, 1957). Further incidents prompted rioting in early 1953.

Initial Repatriation Phase

According to Article 118 of the Third Geneva Convention, "prisoners of war shall be released and repatriated without delay after the cessation of active hostilities" (Geneva Convention Relative to the Treatment of Prisoners of War, 1949). The repatriation of prisoners was a significant issue in the armistice talks—indeed, one of the reasons a treaty was never signed to conclude the war. When armistice talks began, North Korean and Chinese officials wanted their citizens and soldiers returned, but many held by the Allies did not wish to return. South Korea also did not want to force any Koreans to return to the North against their will. The UN Command decided in January 1952 that prisoners should be able to decide for themselves whether to repatriate. This was a continuing point of contention in the talks (Summers, 1990).[2]

As Table 3.2 indicates, among both communist and noncommunist prisoners there were those who wished to be repatriated and those

---

[2]   The Fourth Geneva Convention provides a nonrefoulement provision for interned civilians who do not wish to be repatriated, and a nonrefoulement provision is deemed to be implicit in the Third Convention (Pictet, 1960).

Table 3.2
Prisoner and Repatriation Categories

Desire to Repatriate	Prisoner Type	
	Communist	Noncommunist
Yes	Included hard-core North Korean communists and Chinese communist officers; also included South Korean communists seeking to go to North Korea	Included North Koreans and Chinese who wanted to see their families again and were not particularly political, perhaps because they had been conscripted
No	Included North Koreans who participated in CI&E activities or who had been pressed into service and captured and now feared reprisal. Most either did not have families or did not care if they saw them again.	Included South Korean soldiers captured by North Korea and forced to fight in South Korea as well as South Korean civilians who had been inadvertently captured by U.S. forces

who did not. Indeed, screening and rescreening by U.S. forces found that only one in five Chinese and two in five North Koreans wished to repatriate (White, 1957).

As prisoner administration increasingly focused on questions of repatriation, prisoner education programs became more narrowly focused. The May 1952 hostage-taking of the camp commander at Koje-do had made it impossible to continue prisoner education there. After Operation SCATTER, the CI&E field operating division office moved to Pusan and redistributed its equipment to camps with non-repatriating prisoners. Although the UN commander had intended to return CI&E programs to repatriate camps, program administrators ultimately deemed that effort less important than helping South Koreans and Chinese who would stay and live in a democratic society (U.S. Army Pacific Headquarters, 1960).

Operation SCATTER wreaked havoc on the CI&E programs; it was much more difficult to administer or evaluate programs throughout Korea, especially when prisoners were needed to set up the new camps. Nevertheless, CI&E staff reestablished the political orientation program for all prisoners who were not repatriating and ran literacy training, school continuation, agriculture, health, and other programs as quickly as resource availability permitted. Table 3.3 shows the number of participants in these repatriation-phase programs.

The goal of these programs was the same as those of the initial program: to keep prisoners occupied so as to minimize unrest, to assist them in becoming self-sufficient on some work projects, and to help them learn basic facts about democracy, specifically those counter to communist propaganda (U.S. Army Pacific Headquarters, 1960). Closer to the time of release, CI&E administrators offered five days of concentrated instruction, including film and radio programs.

Final Repatriation Phase

In June 1953, China, North Korea, and the UN Command agreed to allow a neutral party, India, to take custody of North Korean and Chinese prisoners who refused to return home. The Indian Army was to hold these prisoners in the Demilitarized Zone for 120 days while an independent commission ensured that they indeed did not want to return. This plan was thwarted, in part, when South Korean guards released more than 27,000 North Korean prisoners on June 18, 1953.

Table 3.3
CI&E Program Participants, May 1952 to June 1953

Activity	Number of Participants
Orientation on democracy	69,998
Literacy	11,307
Juvenile education	3,525
Adult continuing education	3,958
Reading and literacy groups	42,000
Agriculture	13,674
Health	15,007
Vocational classes	2,577
Vocational production	1,994

Remaining North Korean prisoners not wishing to repatriate moved to two camps where CI&E programs were limited to loudspeaker broadcasting. The full CI&E program continued at the camp of Chinese prisoners not wishing to repatriate.

Before the Indian Army took custody of those not wishing to repatriate, the CI&E loudspeaker broadcasts focused on helping prisoners prepare for life within the Demilitarized Zone. The broadcasts apprised prisoners of relevant developments and reassured them of their security. U.S. and South Korean officers and civilians tried to solve prisoner problems through plans with names such as REASSURANCE and EXPLANATION. Among other plans, COOPERATION reminded prisoners of the good treatment they had received from the UN Command, INTERIM stressed opportunities in the free world for those not repatriating, and FREEDOM explained the details of truce talks and the armistice agreement. These efforts ended when the Indian Army assumed custody of the remaining prisoners, with CI&E administrators letting prisoners keep course materials (U.S. Army Pacific Headquarters, 1960).

Prisoner operations concluded with Operation BIG SWITCH in August 1953, when the UN Command exchanged 76,000 detainees for 12,700 UN prisoners held by North Korea. Prisoners and detainees did their best to destroy all means of conveyance during their movement north. An additional 22,600 prisoners, both Chinese and Korean, who did not want to be repatriated were transferred to Indian Army control in September 1953 (Gebhardt, 2005).

Conclusions

That Allied forces were able to house, feed, and generally care for nearly 200,000 prisoners was impressive, especially considering the speed and intensity of battle and the dramatic changes in fortune during the war. Nevertheless, even camps near "perfection," as the Red Cross described them, could not prevent battles from erupting behind the wire.

U.S. Army Intelligence was not prepared to screen prisoners who spoke a different language, were illiterate, and carried no identification.

The U.S. Army did not have enough trained guards and had to rely on South Korean guards to maintain security. The scale of the job led to an initial disregard for reaching "hearts and minds" in favor of providing food and shelter. When the war came to a stalemate, it moved into the camps, which had been infiltrated by communist and anticommunist agitators.

The education and information programs were seemingly successful. Nevertheless, while many prisoners benefited from the programs, especially the literacy, agriculture, and news programs, the overall program itself also increased the polarization of the prisoners.

The Korean experience, like the German one before it, demonstrated the importance of being able to screen large numbers of prisoners using their languages. Screening prisoners by ideological category, as also eventually occurred in World War II, may prove helpful, although it might also prove problematic, should ideological groups cohere and seek violence against others.

As it did with German prisoners in World War II, providing factual information to prisoners during the Korean War helped dispel rumors, anti-U.S. propaganda, and fear of the United States. Prisoners warmed to the United States and Western democracy as they learned more about it.

The Korean War detainee experience also showed that providing education programs without providing a clear resolution to prisoner status can lead to problems. As prisoners (most of whom are quite young) study and learn, they become more interested in their future and the future of their country. This can cause them to want to become more actively involved in the conflict, making them susceptible to polarizing groups. This would be evident in future conflicts more nebulous than this conventional war.

CHAPTER FOUR

Prisoner and Detainee Operations in Vietnam

Even though the U.S. and Allied forces had designed, built, and implemented prisoner camps and reeducation programs during World War II and the Korean War, many of the lessons learned from managing prisoners in the earlier conflicts were not immediately transferred to the Vietnam conflict. In Vietnam, the U.S. military faced many of the same challenges it had in the past, including

- lack of initial planning for handling massive numbers of prisoners
- inability to correctly identify prisoners as communists, anticommunists, civilians, or insurgents
- lack of cultural, sociological, political, and economic understanding of enemy prisoners
- difficulty of applying the 1949 Geneva Conventions for handling prisoners and civilians.

Nevertheless, the conduct of prisoner and detainee operations during the Vietnam War differed from those in the Korean War and World War II in at least three significant ways:

- The United States did not directly maintain and administer prisoner internment facilities. Rather, it turned detainees over to South Vietnamese authorities while assisting the establishment and administration of detainee centers.
- Particularly before 1972, the Vietnam conflict was primarily an insurgency and not a conventional war.

- There was an earlier recognition that the outcome of the war and the post-conflict environment could be favorably shaped if a better understanding of the enemy was developed. Leveraging the availability of the detainee population for interviews, military planners and detention officials were able to develop and refine their strategies for counterinsurgency.

Categorization of Prisoners of War and Detainees

Though no formal system was used to classify detainees during the Vietnam conflict, detainees comprised three distinct categories:

- uniformed personnel openly engaging in military actions, whether of the Viet Cong or the North Vietnamese Army
- sympathizers, collaborators, infiltrators, spies, or other clandestine supporters of the insurgency, who were neither uniformed nor engaged in direct military action
- defectors who wished to rejoin the side of the South Vietnamese government.

Much of the difficulty in determining the appropriate program for prisoners and detainees lay in determining their status, specifically determining which prisoners and detainees were truly enemy POWs covered by the Third Geneva Convention. The United States and South Vietnam treated only those individuals captured while engaging in direct military action as enemy POWs.

There were also programs for captured spies, terrorists, and saboteurs not known to be involved in direct military actions. Though not directly part of detainee operations, these do offer lessons and insights on handling detainees, particularly in a counterinsurgency. The Chieu Hoi (roughly translated as "Open Arms") program encouraged defection from the Viet Cong and the North Vietnamese Army. The Phung Hoang ("Phoenix") program sought to identify and neutralize—that is, render ineffective or incapable of military action—the clandestine support of the Viet Cong.

Like that for the Vietnam War as a whole, there is still ongoing controversy about these programs. We do not seek to contribute to this debate as much as we seek to present a basic overview of these programs and the lessons they may offer for subsequent detainee operations. The implementation of the prisoner program helps illustrate how the U.S. military dealt with these issues in a complex and unconventional war environment—an environment more closely resembling conflicts in recent years. The additional programs help illustrate previous issues the U.S. military has faced in a counterinsurgency and perhaps can offer lessons on the most effective means of positively shaping detainee motivations. They also help illustrate the importance of targeting the clandestine infrastructure of an insurgency and the need to devise detainee operations that can help develop key sources of intelligence.

We also present an overview of the motivation and morale study RAND conducted regarding captured Viet Cong and North Vietnamese personnel and how such research can be adapted to future operations.

Application of the Geneva Conventions and Detention of Insurgents

When the first large contingent of U.S. ground troops entered Vietnam in 1965, they encountered a chaotic situation. The South Vietnamese government faced a growing insurgency that was increasingly difficult to contain. It treated all detainees, whether Viet Cong fighters, sympathizers, or North Vietnamese soldiers, as political prisoners, subject neither to the rule of law nor the Geneva Conventions. As U.S. troops engaged and captured insurgents and Northern infiltrators, they turned prisoners over to the South Vietnamese government.

This policy came under increasing strain, especially as the U.S. military sought better treatment for its troops captured by the Viet Cong or the North Vietnamese. The North Vietnamese announced that it would treat any U.S. airmen it captured as "air pirates" and neither grant them POW status nor extend to them Geneva Convention protections for prisoners. Reports of inhumane treatment soon surfaced, including the public parading of detainees, solitary confinement (continuing for several years in some cases), and inadequate medical care (U.S. Senate Committee on the Judiciary, 1972). In 1965, the National Liberation Front (NLF) executed three U.S. servicemen in retaliation for the South Vietnamese killing of terrorists (Gebhardt, 2005).[1] The U.S. government sought to grant POW status to both Viet Cong and North Vietnamese prisoners in order to put pressure on the North Vietnamese to improve treatment of American servicemen. In addition, both the International Committee of the Red Cross and Western public opinion recoiled at the abuses of prisoners committed by the South Vietnamese, abuses seen at least as partly the responsibility of the United States, the main supporter of the South's effort to contain the insurgency. Indeed, Article 12 of the Third Geneva Convention holds the power that detained prisoners responsible for their treatment even if it transfers those prisoners to another power. The U.S. military therefore sought to implement a comprehensive prisoner program as part of its military effort in Vietnam.

One key issue that the United States faced in implementing this policy was whether the conflict was international or internal to Vietnam, which in turn affected the applicability of the Geneva Conventions. The United States recognized the South Vietnamese government (but not the North Vietnamese) and recognized that North Vietnam was a party to the Geneva Conventions. The United States maintained that "the hostilities constituted an armed international conflict, that North Vietnam was a belligerent, that the Viet Cong were agents of the government of North Vietnam," and that therefore the Geneva Conventions were fully applicable (Prugh, 1975, p. 63). The North Vietnamese contended that the conflict was an internal one and further claimed that the Geneva Conventions were not applicable because war had not been declared.[2] Indeed, neither the United States nor North

---

[1]   The NLF was organized as the official political-military vehicle in South Vietnam for overthrowing the U.S.-allied South Vietnamese government. Although it contained non-Communist nationalists, its leadership was dominated by the Communist Workers' Party (Lao Dong).

[2]   Nevertheless, Article 2 of the Third Geneva Convention states that the Convention applies "to all cases of declared war or of any other armed conflict which may arise between

Vietnam ever made a declaration of war regarding the conflict. South Vietnam did declare a state of emergency in 1964 and a state of war in 1965, but this was done primarily to gain more legal leeway in dealing with growing unrest.[3]

Even if the South Vietnamese had sought to treat prisoners properly, it remained the case that they lacked suitable facilities for confining them (Prugh, 1975).[4] Some detention facilities lacked the resources to feed or manage their prisoners. By housing all prisoners together, not only were South Vietnamese officials violating the Fourth Geneva Convention, requiring civilian internees, POWs, and regular criminal or administrative detainees to be housed and administered separately, but they were also giving the Viet Cong a chance to foment resentment, proselytize, and recruit among other prisoners. These problems were exacerbated as the detainee population grew. During 1965, the number of political prisoners the South Vietnamese held nearly doubled, from 9,895 to 18,786. The total capacity of all civilian jails and prisons in South Vietnam was 21,400, so, assuming that the jails and prisons were otherwise empty, by 1966 there was little or no room for additional detainees. At this point, the detention centers effectively became a revolving door; as new prisoners came in, others had to be discharged. In 1965, 24,878 political prisoners passed through the detention facilities, and 15,987 were released. The average time of

---

two or more of the High Contracting Parties, even if the state of war is not recognized by one of them that its provisions are applicable, even if the state of war is not recognized by one of the participants," as well as to occupations (Geneva Convention Relative to the Treatment of Prisoners of War, 1949). Even if the war was truly intrastate, Article 3, common to all of the Geneva Conventions and providing basic protections, would have applied, but it appears North Vietnam did not apply it either.

[3]   By formally declaring a state of war, the South Vietnamese government could undertake extraordinary measures to deal with the growing unrest and chaos, such as promulgating decree-laws that limited civil liberties and establishing stiff penalties for supporting the Viet Cong (Prugh, 1975).

[4]   Article 3 of the Third Geneva Convention stipulates, "Prisoners of war shall be quartered under conditions as favorable as those for the forces of the Detaining Power who are billeted in the same area."

confinement for all prisoners, including Viet Cong, was six months (Andradé, 1990).[5]

This situation, had it continued, would have had catastrophic consequences. No one could have been expected to collaborate in identifying Viet Cong supporters only to see such supporters released in a few months or even weeks and able to exact revenge on government collaborators. Likewise, it would have been difficult, if not impossible, to weaken the insurgency if its fighters and supporters were not incapacitated by detention or incarceration.

The Enemy Prisoner of War Program

Treatment of prisoners and detainees began to change with the establishment of an enemy POW program (Prugh, 1975). The U.S. Secretary of State informed the International Committee of the Red Cross in August 1965 that the United States would apply all provisions of the Geneva Conventions in Vietnam and expected other parties to do the same. South Vietnam agreed the next day, but North Vietnam instead threatened to prosecute U.S. pilots under its civilian criminal laws (a threat it never actually carried out).[6] In October 1965, the Chairman of the Joint Chiefs of Staff directed his staff to examine POW policy and practices in Vietnam and the application of the Geneva Conventions. Later that same month, the Red Cross informed the U.S. Secretary of State that South Vietnam was not complying with the Geneva Conventions and that the Red Cross would continue to hold the United States responsible for prisoners it turned over to the South Vietnamese government (Gebhardt, 2005).

---

[5]   While POWs may be held until the end of hostilities, the Fourth Geneva Convention provides that civilian internees should be released after six months unless a review board finds it absolutely necessary to continue to hold them.

[6]   One of the purposes of POW status is to immunize military service members from criminal prosecution for acts of violence that are legalized in warfare.

In order both to apply the Geneva Conventions and to correct ongoing problems in managing prisoner populations, the U.S. military implemented a series of steps, including

- a formal plan to immediately begin application of the Geneva Conventions to all individuals captured by American, Vietnamese, and allied forces. All detainees would be given POW status while their ultimate status was determined.
- issuing guidance, starting in October 1965, to troops in the field on "The Enemy in Your Hands," coupled with a program of instruction for both U.S. and Vietnamese forces on the principles and rules governing the treatment of POWs
- most importantly, to handle the unexpectedly large number of detainees, construction of five POW camps, each with an initial capacity of 1,000, manned by South Vietnamese military police with U.S. military police as advisors. In 1967, the combined capacity of these camps was increased to 13,000. In 1968, two additional camps were built, and the combined capacity of all camps increased to 21,000 or up to 32,000 on an emergency or temporary basis. By the end of 1971, South Vietnam held 35,665 prisoners, one-third of whom had been captured by U.S. forces (Prugh, 1975).

The Military Assistance Command, Vietnam (MACV) complemented these efforts with a March 1966 directive defining four categories of detainees whose status had not yet been determined. These were

- POWs—individuals captured in combat who would be promptly transferred to a POW camp
- civil defendants—individuals who had been captured under circumstances not warranting their treatment as POWs, including terrorists, spies, saboteurs, and suspected members of the clandestine Viet Cong infrastructure, turned over to civil or local security authorities

- returnees—individuals who voluntarily returned to the control of the South Vietnamese government, also known as "ralliers," who were placed in the Chieu Hoi program
- innocent civilians, who were to be released immediately and, if possible, returned to their point of capture.

These policies failed to persuade the Viet Cong and the North Vietnamese to apply the Geneva Conventions to the prisoners they held. They also failed to earn legitimacy in world opinion. Nevertheless, they did earn praise from the Red Cross as "a brilliant expression of a liberal and realistic attitude [that] goes far beyond the requirements of the Geneva Convention" (Prugh, 1975, p. 68). Yet the emphasis on prisoner programs was coupled with a "total disregard for civilian prisons to house convicted" Viet Cong—a result, one historian contended, "of the military's misunderstanding of the nature of the war" (Andradé, 1990).

Detainee Operations

Though not as formally developed as the prisoner programs, two counterinsurgency programs, Chieu Hoi and Phung Hoang, both played significant roles in efforts to pacify Vietnam. As noted, Chieu Hoi sought to encourage defection from the insurgency, while Phung Hoang sought to neutralize the infrastructure supporting it. The programs were complementary; indeed, one historian writes, Chieu Hoi was often the largest producer of intelligence for executing the Phung Hoang program, with some Chieu Hoi participants even participating as interrogators in the Phung Hoang program (Andradé, 1990). Likewise, the more effective Phung Hoang, the greater the number of defectors who sought the Chieu Hoi program. Indeed, after a particularly effective pacification campaign against the Viet Cong in Quang Dien in late 1968, the number of defectors to the Chieu Hoi program increased dramatically.

Phung Hoang: Targeting the Infrastructure

Contrary to popular belief, the Phung Hoang program was never meant to be an assassination scheme but rather a way to pool intelligence sources and focus them in an effort to dismantle the infrastructure supporting the Viet Cong (Hunt, 1998). In some cases, when actionable intelligence revealed the location of important Viet Cong personnel, Phung Hoang involved direct action seeking the capture or death of the target. Nevertheless, as Table 4.1 shows, most of those neutralized under Phung Hoang were not killed. Rather, between 1968 and 1972, 64 percent of those targeted by Phung Hoang were captured or rallied to the South Vietnamese cause.

Drawing lessons from the Malayan "Troubles," the Huk Rebellion in the Philippines, and even the French experience in Indochina, the program, initially known as infrastructure coordination and exploitation (ICEX), sought to turn pacification into a main part of the war effort.[7] The effort increased as it became clear that disman-

Table 4.1
Phung Hoang Neutralization Result

Year	Rallied	Captured	Killed	Total
1968	2,229	11,288	2,259	15,776
1969	4,832	8,515[a]	6,187	11,019
1970	7,745	6,405	8,191	22,341
1971	5,621	5,012	7,057	17,690
1972 (end of July)	1,586	2,138	2,675	6,399
Total	22,013	24,843	26,369	73,225

SOURCE: Andradé, 1990.
[a] Beginning in 1969, only Viet Cong receiving sentences of one year or more were counted as captured.

---

[7]   For example, similar to the incentives offered to ralliers in South Vietnam, former Huk guerillas in the Philippines received a reeducation program on the benefits of rejoining society and also received a plot of land to work. As the program succeeded, applicants soon outnumbered available plots, and it was expanded. For more on counterinsurgency in the Huk rebellion, see Greenberg, 1987.

tling the Viet Cong infrastructure was an important component of the counterinsurgency.

ICEX originated from a July 1967 MACV directive and was placed under the direct supervision of the Civil Operations and Rural Development Support (CORDS) Program (Andradé, 1990). CORDS brought under one umbrella all the counterinsurgency programs run by the military, the Central Intelligence Agency, the United States Agency for International Development, the United States Information Agency, and other smaller civilian agencies working in Vietnam (Krepinevich, 1986). Phung Hoang became the primary source of assistance given by CORDS to the police in their efforts to suppress the Viet Cong infrastructure.

A program such as Phung Hoang depends on the ability of the government to accurately identify members of the insurgency infrastructure and to convict and secure those it identifies. Unfortunately, the South Vietnamese government was unable or unwilling to do either of these tasks effectively. The Public Safety Division of CORDS asked the South Vietnamese government to establish a tamperproof national identification system, which it was not able to do. Widespread bribery and use of aliases limited government attempts to track and incarcerate Viet Cong members.

Similarly, South Vietnam did not institute effective civilian courts and prisons to support the Phung Hoang program. This, some contended, reflected an emphasis on conventional war over counterinsurgency and pacification efforts. One historian contended that the "MACV was content to watch political prisoners swell provincial jails, never admitting that although they had the POWs well in hand, the most important enemy," the Viet Cong, "was not being adequately handled within the detention system" (Andradé, 1990, p. 209). Indeed, as noted earlier, the jails holding the Viet Cong often held them for only short periods of time because of insufficient space.

The lack of adequate detainment facilities in particular and of a functioning rule of law in general led to inconsistent handling of detainees. A member of the Viet Cong, if captured in combat, was treated as a POW and sent to a prisoner camp, where he would likely be confined for the length of the war. This same member, if captured by police in a city or village search, would likely be sent to a reeducation center, where he would be treated as a common criminal without the protections of the Geneva Conventions, but would likely be released in a few months without trial (Prugh, 1975).

Chieu Hoi: Using Defection Programs in a Counterinsurgency

Programs aimed at fostering defection usually play an integral part in a counterinsurgency. Vietnam was no exception. Chieu Hoi, instituted in 1963, became one of the few programs that showed continuity over time in the Vietnam conflict (Koch, 1973). Focused primarily on the Viet Cong, the U.S. Army's Chieu Hoi program encouraged defection by means of propaganda, usually leaflets delivered by artillery shell or dropped by aircraft over enemy-controlled areas in South Vietnam. In the decade that followed its implementation, about 194,000 guerillas participated in the program. Chieu Hoi provided ralliers, also known as Hoi Chanh, an alternative to the hardships of guerrilla life and an opportunity to rejoin society and receive a legal pardon and even vocational training.

In its early years, Chieu Hoi was one of the most efficient programs to convert rebels to the South Vietnamese cause. Between 1963 and 1965, the program had a per capita cost of only $14 for each of the 27,789 ralliers it attracted, prompting the United States to devote more resources and personnel to it.[8] Nevertheless, South Vietnamese were not very enthusiastic and gave the program a lower priority. In 1966, cooperation between the United States and South Vietnam in the program improved, and the number of ralliers doubled. In 1967, Chieu Hoi became a ministry of the South Vietnamese government and came under the responsibility of CORDS. The Tet Offensive of 1968 robbed the program of some momentum, but in 1969 it reached its greatest number of ralliers, 47,023. In 1970, the program placed more emphasis on convincing specific, higher-level members of the Viet Cong to rally, particularly through the use of armed propaganda teams who personally distributed Chieu Hoi propaganda in contested areas or areas con-

---

[8]   Koch (1973) also notes that at its peak year, 1969, the per capita cost had increased to $350, while adding that budget numbers for different years are not strictly comparable.

trolled by the Viet Cong. In subsequent years, the program withered as U.S. involvement in the war waned.

Initiatives such as Chieu Hoi seek both a military and political impact. They not only reduce the ranks of insurgents but also send the message that even once-ardent supporters of the insurgency can become disenchanted. As one analysis of the movement noted, "the political implication of 194,000 of the enemy defecting . . . in some degree reflects a loss of political faith, of confidence in victory, or of personal motivation" (Koch, 1973, p. 107).

Programs aimed at inducing defection among insurgents have a twofold advantage: They are cost-effective, and they can foster reconciliation and rehabilitation. The main shortcoming of Chieu Hoi was an initial lack of commitment by the South Vietnamese government. This led to systematic underfunding, understaffing, and an overall lack of political will to realize the program's potential. As a result, an analysis of the program found, "the political rehabilitation of the rallier has been generally inadequate" (Koch, 1973, p. 110). Gradually, Chieu Hoi received greater recognition. An analysis of the program found

> The initial reluctance on the part of most Vietnamese to accept this "American program" has gradually given way to some recognition that only through the ultimate re-absorption of the thousands of their own fellow Vietnamese now on the enemy side can the political war be won. (Koch, 1973, p. 10)

Administrators also made the program more effective by hiring Chieu Hoi participants to fill administrative positions and more politically aware Hoi Chanh as instructors. This made the program a source of employment for former insurgents, helping avoid the apprehension most employers would have about hiring such persons.

Still, a perception persisted that the program did little but offer participants a respite before rejoining the insurgency (Long, 2006; Russo, 1972). The lack of follow-up with ralliers was one possible reason for this perception because there was no way to determine how many ralliers were re-recruited by the Viet Cong. The program also had very little success with high-level Viet Cong leaders and, particularly, North Vietnamese soldiers (Long, 2006). Among the 47,023 ralliers that joined Chieu Hoi in 1969, for example, only 368 were North Vietnamese soldiers (Koch, 1973).

Motivation and Morale

The American war in Vietnam was, as Robert McNamara called it, "a social scientists' war" in which a loose network of policy-oriented social scientists moved between government, academe, and "think tanks" to help establish the intellectual underpinning for the U.S. counterinsurgency effort in Indochina (Marquis, 2000). Part of this effort included the RAND Corporation's Viet Cong Motivation and Morale Project, undertaken for the Department of Defense (DoD) in the mid-1960s.

The RAND study proposed an examination of "the structure of the Viet Cong organization and the motivations of those who supported it" in response to "expressions of interest of officials in the Defense and State Departments" (Davison, 1972, p. 1). Between August 1964 and December 1968, RAND researchers supervised South Vietnamese subcontractors who conducted approximately 2,400 interviews, primarily with defectors from the NLF and prisoners captured from the North Vietnamese Army. The 62,000 pages of transcripts from these interviews formed the basis for a series of reports on the ideological commitment of NLF supporters, the NLF response to South Vietnamese and U.S. military pressure, the political structure in the Communist-controlled Dinh Tuong province of South Vietnam, and the impact of the war in battle zones (Davison, 1972; Landau, 1972; Russo, 1972). This study sheds light on the potential benefits that can be reaped from interviewing detainees, as well as the pitfalls of using such sources.

Some critics of the Motivation and Morale Project contended that the results were biased because respondents were mostly defectors from the communist cause, South Vietnamese interviewers were predisposed to take a hostile position toward the communists, and RAND researchers in Vietnam could not function as independent scholars because they "cooperated closely with American and Saigon military personnel, whose good will was essential in day-to-day operations" (Hunt, 1974). At the same time, RAND researchers contended that the study could just as plausibly overestimate communist strengths, given that defectors could exaggerate their role or commitment if they felt interviewers wished to hear such claims. RAND analysts attempted to control for biases of interviewers and interview subjects by checking answers for internal consistency and comparing interview data with other sources of information, yielding, they believed, a balanced view (Davison, 1972).

Project leaders and interviewers found defectors easier to query than captives but also noted variations within these two groups. Some seemed eager to please the interviewer by overstating sentiment against the Viet Cong, while others seemed like infiltrators attempting to proselytize (Davison, 1972).

The Motivation and Morale study in Vietnam showed that insurgents' military power and resources did not appear to have much effect on their morale. The Viet Cong were grossly outnumbered and outgunned by the United States, yet their morale seemed unshaken. North Vietnamese and Viet Cong soldiers had internalized the political ends for which they fought, assimilating and rendering them in their own terms illustrated by personal examples and experiences (Kellen, 1970).

RAND's Motivation and Morale study was a pioneering effort in its attempt to understand the adversary's perspective. Classic interrogations usually pursue facts and aim to discover who the prisoner is, what he knows, what he has done, or what he intends to do. Broader questions aim to tap into his knowledge and find out what the enemy is doing, what plans are in the making, and where troops are located. The Motivation and Morale study attempted to understand the adversary's perceptions and level of determination. It sought to understand his will and values. This knowledge is crucial for the conduct of any war, and especially so when facing unconventional and asymmetric adversaries. Only when understanding "what makes them fight" can the U.S. military direct its best efforts to making them stop. Without such understanding, effective plans, strategies, and policies at countering such opponents are not possible.

Conclusions

The Vietnam War, as the largest U.S. counterinsurgency campaign prior to the Iraq war, offers several lessons for other, similar efforts. These lessons include both blunders and shortcomings to avoid and some moderate successes to replicate.

Complex and asymmetrical conflicts such as Vietnam will generally lead to the need to detain combatant POWs, civilian internees, and civilian criminal defendants—perhaps in large numbers. In the early stages of planning for military operations, it is imperative to devise adequate processes and facilities for these groups and formally develop doctrine for uniformly treating them in a manner consistent with international standards.

Leveraging detainee availability for interviews in order to gain a better understanding of what motivates and sustains them can be used to shape the battlefield from "behind the wire." Though the detainees' views may not accurately represent those of the entire population, they may represent those who are actively causing instability. Insights drawn from them may not only help defeat the enemy in active combat but also support the peaceful reintegration of detainees into society upon release.

Programs seeking to foster defection among insurgents appeared to offer cost-effective, humane, and sustainable means to weaken an insurgency without having to detain large numbers of insurgents for long periods of time. For a defection program to be successful, it must have pressure accompanying it, such as that Phung Hoang provided Chieu Hoi. Efforts to dismantle the infrastructure of the insurgency and encourage defection should be complementary. To evaluate the success of counterinsurgency programs, it is imperative to have a system to track the activities of defectors after release.

Finally, if the United States steadfastly supports another nation in its counterinsurgency campaign, it should realize that expecting the host nation to bear the primary responsibility for detainee operations in compliance with accepted human rights covenants may be unrealistic. The United States is likely to be held responsible or equally culpable for the actions of the host nation. Hence, persuading host nations to commit to adequate action is an important part of the planning process for detainee operations in a counterinsurgency. If the host nation is not able, the United States will have to fill that role.

CHAPTER FIVE
Detainee Operations in Iraq

The preceding chapters have outlined prisoner and detainee operations in a variety of circumstances, each with lessons for the conflicts of today. German prisoners in World War II were taken in a conventional conflict and trained to have a role in the reconstruction of their homeland. This occurred despite some misgivings that the German "national character" could not be adapted to democracy. Korean War prisoners were taken in a civil war and trained to develop basic skills that could serve them in a democratic society. Vietnam War prisoners and detainees were taken in a conflict involving conventional and unconventional forces, in what was in essence an insurrection, with efforts made to convince them to defect. Each of these conflicts offers lessons for comparable situations in present-day conflicts. These include ways of better understanding and classifying the prisoners for their own safety, influencing them in ways that will decrease their adversarial sentiments and intentions, and fostering skills and attitudes that can help after the conflict.

As in previous conflicts, planners did not foresee the eventual scope of detention operations in Iraq. The military invasion of Iraq began on March 20, 2003, and the Coalition declared the invasion complete by April 30, 2003. Cast as an intervention to overthrow a repressive regime, this action was not thought to require any significant prisoner operations. This perception would soon require revision.

49

Those in charge of detainee operations in the Iraq war faced many of the problems common to earlier conflicts, as well as some which were unique to the Iraqi environment.[1] These included

- underdeveloped doctrine that did not adequately reflect the lessons learned from previous detainee operations and could not be uniformly applied across the Iraq theater
- challenges interpreting and applying the Coalition's authority to detain, as granted by the Coalition Provisional Authority (CPA) and the United Nations Security Council
- inadequate pre-conflict planning for handling large numbers of detainees and, on realization that a large-scale counterinsurgency was yielding a large number of detainees, difficulty in forecasting the required capacity and obtaining funds to build adequate facilities
- inadequate coordination and information sharing between those who capture the detainees and those who house and release detainees
- insufficient numbers of qualified personnel, including interrogators, linguists, and guards. Detention personnel were primarily drawn from military police companies trained in standard law enforcement but not familiar with detainee operations or counterinsurgency strategies and tactics
- inadequate cultural, sociological, political, and economic understanding of enemy detainees
- delays in recognizing the significance of the detainee issue and in developing appropriate programs to influence the ongoing battle and the political process
- a looming expectation that the Coalition would lose the authority to detain and would be forced to release thousands of detainees to the GOI, a government then incapable of adequately managing such an influx of detainees.

---

[1]   The description and analysis of the Iraq detention effort, as presented in this monograph, reflect the views and experiences of TF-134 commanders and officers, as related to RAND researchers, and the observations of the RAND team, which provided direct support to TF-134 over the period of a year.

As time passed, Iraqi detainee operations did incorporate some of the successes of earlier detainee operations, particularly those of training, assessing the motivations of the detainee population, and updating doctrine to reflect a shift in the way military operations are conducted in the face of asymmetric threats.

In this chapter, as in earlier ones, we discuss various challenges and emerging solutions to detainee operations. The organization directly responsible for detention operations in Iraq, Task Force (TF) 134, allowed RAND researchers largely unrestricted access to their facilities, current and former personnel, and data. Therefore, our assessment of Iraq detainee operations is considerably more detailed than those of earlier chapters. We address the major challenges faced by managing detainees from spring 2003 through mid-2008, a period encompassing the toppling of Saddam Hussein's regime, the Abu Ghraib prisoner abuse scandal, the height of the insurgency against Coalition forces and the GOI, and the surge in forces intended to quell the insurgency. We present an overview of detainee operations, including how they evolved as the focus of U.S. military operations shifted from major combat operations to supporting the CPA and Iraqi sovereignty.

Legal and Doctrinal Issues Associated with the Iraq Experience

By late 2003, as the U.S. military shifted from major combat operations to stability operations, its detainee operations also shifted from managing enemy POWs—i.e., soldiers of an enemy state's military— to managing other types of detainees.

On June 18, 2003, the CPA issued CPA Memorandum No. 3 (Criminal Procedures), establishing policy for detention operations after major combat operations had ended. This memorandum distinguishes between detainees held for reasons of security and those held for criminal activities. Security detainees were to receive an administrative hearing within six months of internment, based on the Fourth Geneva Convention rules for internees. Criminal detainees were to be given to Iraqi authorities for prosecution in Iraqi courts.

The Coalition forces, hoping to minimize the number of unwarranted detentions, established a series of reviews at three successive levels: capturing unit, theater internment facility, and the Iraqi-U.S. Combined Review Board. If evidence warranted, detainees also could be transferred to the Iraqi criminal justice system. The Coalition's detainee operations command required review of a detainee's status after 18 months in detention, resulting either in release or, with joint Coalition and Iraqi approval, continuation of the detention for another 18 months. Juveniles less than 18 years of age could be held for a maximum of 12 months, after which they had to be released, unless there was sufficient evidence to remand them to Iraqi criminal courts.

With the reemergence of Iraq as a sovereign nation on June 28, 2004, the UN Security Council issued Resolution (UNSCR) 1546, codifying an agreement between the United States, the Interim Iraqi Government, and the UN Security Council that transformed the nature of the Coalition forces' presence in Iraq from invader and occupier to requested force multiplier. The Coalition presence in Iraq was reorganized with the dissolution of the CPA and Combined Joint Task Force 7 (CJTF-7), by a permanent U.S. Embassy and a newly formed Multi-National Force–Iraq (MNF-I), and the Multi-National Corps–Iraq (MNC-I), the subordinate command within the MNF-I responsible for most combat operations.

MNF-I was given control over detention operations and was tasked with helping Iraq rebuild its judicial, correctional, and law enforcement system. Within MNF-I, TF-134 assumed direct control over detainee operations.

Prior to its dissolution, the CPA revised Memorandum No. 3 to apply the Fourth Geneva Convention to future detainee operations. The CPA memorandum also provided a review process for detainees reiterating the distinction between security and criminal detainees. (See the appendix for a more-detailed summary of the MNF-I's legal authority to detain.)

Although the CPA had set policy and established legal guidelines for detainee operations, military policy for such operations remained outdated. The breadth of lessons learned from previous conflicts was not adequately reflected in extant doctrine. In some ways, this was a

result of coincidental events. Shortly before the September 2001 terrorist attacks against the United States, the Army published a field
manual governing internment and resettlement operations by military
police, but, like previous doctrine, its focus was largely limited to providing safe housing, food, and medical care to detainees—the traditional "care-and-custody" role.

Successive Army field manuals (3-07.22 and 3-24) gave little
attention to detainee operations.[2] Though the Army made subsequent
attempts to address the detainee problem, by the time a *comprehensive* joint publication on detainees was published in May 2008 (Joint
Chiefs of Staff, 2008), many of the most critical issues had already been
faced and addressed without the help of official guidance.[3]

A Rocky Start for Detainee Operations in Iraq

In June 2003, Brigadier General Janis Karpinski, an Army reservist,
was given command of the 800th Military Police Brigade. This put
her in charge of all detainees in Iraq. Many of the initial detainees
were held near Baghdad at Abu Ghraib, a facility that had been one of
the more notorious prisons of Saddam Hussein (Hersh, 2004). By late
2003, the Coalition held thousands of prisoners at Abu Ghraib, including security detainees (among whom were a few suspected "high-value"
leaders of the insurgency) as well as criminals.

---

[2] As the Army began to recognize the conflict in Iraq as more of a counterinsurgency operation, it published Army Field Manual—Interim 3-07.22, *Counterinsurgency Operations*, in
late 2004. Yet this publication addressed detainee operations only sparingly, in a very short
(three-page) appendix (I) on "Planning for Detainee Operations and Field Processing of
Detainees." It was regarded as a stopgap measure until Army Field Manual 3-24 could be
published two years later (U.S. Army, 2006b).

[3] In September 2005, the Army published Field Manual—Interim 3-63.6, *Command and
Control of Detainee Operations*. Nevertheless, both the length of the document (seven pages)
and a close review of its contents illustrate that it was a superficial attempt to address only
one segment of the growing "detainee problem." In September 2006, the Deputy Chief of
Staff for Army Intelligence published Field Manual 2-22.3, *Human Intelligence Collector
Operations*. This mentioned detainees only in a seven-page "Guide for Handling Detainees,
Captured Enemy Documents, and Captured Enemy Equipment" (U.S. Army, 2006a).

In August 2003, Major General Geoffrey D. Miller, commanding officer of the detention facility in Guantanamo, Cuba, led a team of staff from Guantanamo to advise Lieutenant General Ricardo Sanchez on how to extract better intelligence from detainees in Iraq. Over Karpinski's objection, policies based on the Guantanamo experience were instituted in Iraq (Mayer, 2008).

Thereafter ensued a period marred by criminal abuse of prisoners at Abu Ghraib, eventually documented by witness statements and photographic evidence. Subsequent official inquiries on the abuses concluded that:

- The primary cause for misconduct was a lack of discipline by leaders and soldiers of the 205th Military Intelligence Brigade and a failure or lack of leadership within CJTF–7 (Jones and Fay, 2004).
- Specific detention or interrogation lessons learned from previous conflicts (including those from the Balkans) were not incorporated into planning for operations in support of the Global War on Terror (Church, 2005).

Other contributors to the abuse included overcrowding of detainees, an underresourced and improperly trained Military Police Brigade, and pressure to obtain actionable intelligence from detainees (Schlesinger et al., 2004; Mayer, 2008).

Following the release of photographs from Abu Ghraib on *60 Minutes* in April 2004, Karpinski was removed from command and replaced by Miller. Miller arrived as riots raged in U.S. internment facilities across Iraq. Allegations that Miller approved of harsh treatment in Guantanamo surfaced shortly after he took command of Iraqi detainee operations, and, like Karpinski before him, he was soon replaced.

The Post–Abu Ghraib Operating Environment

Army Major General William Brandenburg arrived to replace Miller in November 2004. Brandenburg had no detainee operations experience and no adequate doctrine to support his work. Nevertheless, he immediately sought to establish procedures to fix core problems in the detention process (Brandenburg, 2007). At the same time, Washington policymakers had tasked him to begin training Iraqi correctional authorities for an anticipated transfer of detention responsibilities.

By January 2005, Iraqi police were sending prisoners who had committed criminal offenses to overcrowded facilities administered by the Coalition. The Iraqi Ministry of Justice was still in the forming stages and had not yet assumed control over the correctional system. Subsequently, much of Brandenburg's attention focused on interacting with Iraqi authorities regarding the transfer of responsibility for these facilities.

By the spring of 2005, Brandenburg was able to focus more on expanding and improving his own detention facilities for processing a growing number of detainees. Nevertheless, in April 2005 a three-day riot at Camp Bucca, in a remote area of southern Iraq, erupted, in part due to overcrowding and uncertainty among detainees about their status. Through great effort and with a constant struggle to obtain adequate resources, the camp was converted from a tent facility to one with additional compounds, fixed buildings, and a large hospital.

By July 2005, with detainees arriving daily by bus from Abu Ghraib, the population of Camp Bucca swelled to 6,400. More than 3,500 detainees remained at Abu Ghraib, forcing Brandenburg to construct additional housing there. Elsewhere, TF-134 increased capacity at Camp Cropper near Baghdad from 100 to 2,000 by the end of 2005. Brandenburg also oversaw preparations to open a newly refurbished detention facility at Fort Suse in Sulemaniya, 300 miles north of Baghdad. Figure 5.1 shows the location of each of these four Theater Internment Facilities (TIFs).

Brandenburg also sought to improve security within the facilities through a new categorization system. Prior to June 2005, detainees were housed according to their assumed security or risk levels. As

Figure 5.1
Location of Four Theater Internment Facilities in 2005–2006

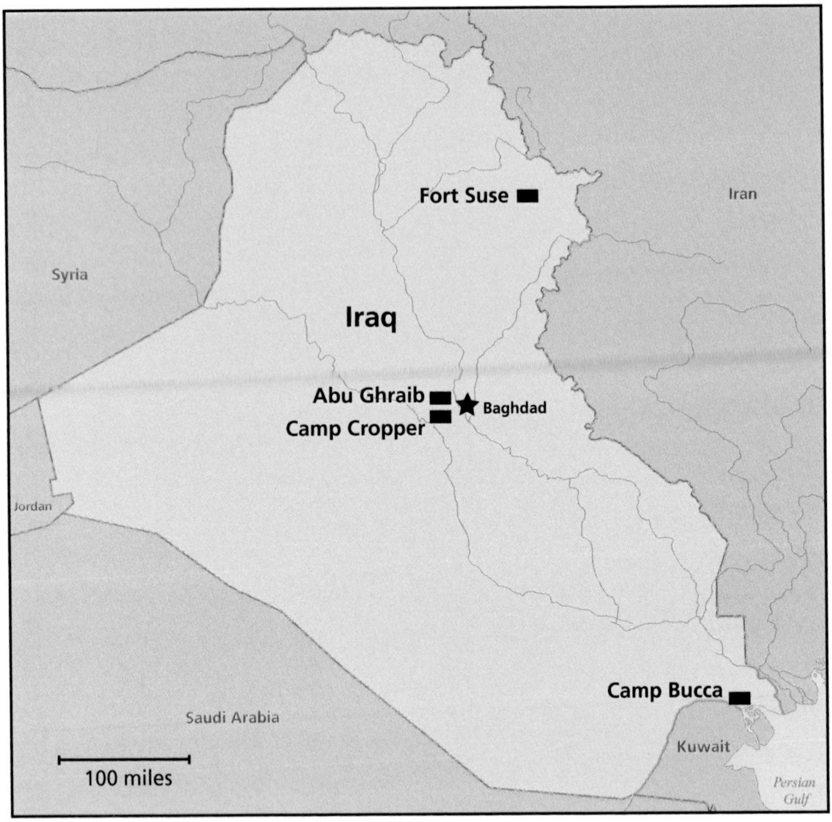

SOURCE: TF-134.

understanding about the sectarian divisions within Iraq grew, TF-134 began categorizing prisoners at Abu Ghraib as "Shia," "Sunni," "Salafist," or "other Muslim."[4]

---

[4] The terms *Salafist, jihadist,* and *Takfiri* were used somewhat loosely by military personnel and others engaged in detainee operations in Iraq. Rightly or wrongly, they were used interchangeably, referring to individuals in custody who followed a violently extremist, radical interpretation of Islam. *Takfiri* refers to individuals who regard their own version of Islam as the only proper one and view those with a more-moderate religious view as not being proper Muslims.

The large numbers of detainees presented such logistical challenges that, initially, their administrators were fully occupied with the task of simply "warehousing" them and accomplishing crude separations of those groups judged most likely to harm or kill each other if housed together. This limited the ability of Brandenburg to implement the more-innovative counterinsurgency and reeducation programs that his successors would later attempt.

Besides logistical challenges, the ability of Brandenburg to improve detention processes also faltered on a "command disconnect," a problem he shared with both his predecessors and his successors (Brandenburg, 2007). Brandenburg, as TF-134 commander, inherited the title of MNF-I Deputy Commanding General for Detainee Operations, but this carried little authority over a vast detention process that extended far beyond the TIFs at Cropper, Bucca, Fort Suse, Abu Ghraib, and the Camp Ashraf Refugee Center. Rather, the Provost Marshal of MNC-I (the operational or battle command under MNF-I), though two grades in rank below the TF-134 commander, oversaw the initial stages of the detention process, including hundreds of detainee collection points and dozens of brigade and division internment facilities across Iraq. This arrangement made it difficult for TF-134 to influence the type of information gathered during initial capture and delayed instituting more-rigorous evidence gathering at the point of capture. Without a way to influence the information gathered in the early stages of detention, TF-134 personnel were sometimes faced with inadequate identifying information about the detainees when they arrived at the TIFs.

A Burgeoning Strategy for Detainee Operations[5]

In December 2005, Army Major General John D. Gardner assumed command of TF-134 (Gardner, 2007).[6] Gardner would serve in this position for 18 months, longer than any TF-134 commander. He

---

[5] The overview of detention operations that follows is based in part on an extensive interview with Major General John Gardner conducted by RAND researchers in 2007.

[6] Gardner was selected for this position only after a personal interview with Donald Rumsfeld. In the wake of the Abu Ghraib scandal and a renewed international focus on detainee operations, the Secretary of Defense wanted to personally interview each TF-134 commander.

arrived having a little experience with prisoners, but none with detainees. As a result, he sought advice from practitioners, including representatives of the Texas Department of Criminal Justice, from whom he sought to learn how to control gang behavior in prison and lessons to apply to Iraq. He also sought his predecessor's advice, seeking "to find out what got the U.S. in trouble and to make sure it didn't happen again" (Gardner, 2007). Brandenburg shared with Gardner his observation that a large number of detainees did not have religious motivations for their actions. Further, he advised that Gardner's first goal should be "to get the U.S. out of detention operations in Iraq" (Gardner, 2007).

Gardner's tenure as commander of detainee operations was characterized by

- a rapid increase in the numbers of detainees held and a commensurate expansion of detention facilities
- introduction of a detainee classification and segregation process
- introduction of programs aimed at deradicalization of extremists, vocational and educational training, and entertainment.

Keeping Pace with Increasing Numbers of Detainees

Trends on the battlefield affected the numbers, types, and motivational composition of detainees that were brought to TF-134. Throughout 2006, al Qaeda in Iraq brought in foreign insurgents whose views were more influenced by the more-extremist interpretations of Islam than those of native Iraqi insurgents. In the sectarian violence following the February 2006 bombing by Sunni insurgents of the Al-Askariya or Golden Dome Mosque, there was a significant increase in the number of detainees, particularly of the Shia Jaysh al-Mahdi militia.

A loosening of requirements for detaining "persons of interest" further increased the number of detainees. By the summer of 2006, battlefield commanders had broader authority to detain persons who were

- engaged in criminal activity
- interfering with mission accomplishment, i.e., sabotaging or deliberately obstructing military efforts

- on a list of persons wanted for questioning regarding criminal or security threats
- among those whose detention was necessary for "imperative reasons of security" (Gardner, 2007).

By early 2006, TF-134 held 13,000 detainees across Iraq, including 4,000 in Abu Ghraib and 7,000 in Camp Bucca. Later in 2006, TF-134 expanded Camp Cropper to hold as many as 3,600 detainees in new hard structures and added five new compounds to Camp Bucca.

Classifying and Adjudicating Detainees

The number of detainees led Gardner to adopt new methods for classifying detainees. The practice of "warehousing" was contributing to growing unrest in the camps. Gardner focused at first on segregating prisoners by religious category. This had two purposes: protecting the prisoners from extremist threats and acts of violence to enforce strict fundamentalist conduct, and reducing the opportunities for agitators to recruit or radicalize their less extremist fellows.

But soon the need for a more-sophisticated method of classifying detainees arose, as Gardner came under pressure to release large numbers of detainees on short notice. The reason was often political, with the order coming at the behest of the Iraqi government. For example, the government announced one large-scale release as a goodwill gesture at the time of the Eid holiday, obliging Gardner to free about 2,000 detainees between February and April 2006 (Gardner, 2007). This raised concerns that some of the more-dangerous detainees might be inadvertently released. Ideally, TF-134 would have had enough information about the detainees to avoid such a possibility, as well as to ensure the appropriate release of detainees not likely to pose future danger. Yet the files on the detainees were in serious disorder; they were incomplete, with information scattered across multiple separate databases. In fact, during this time, TF-134 was unable to account for the files of almost 2,800 detainees. Administrative problems began to replace the issue of abuse as the primary challenge in detainee operations.

To better classify prisoners, in January 2006, Gardner asked the MNF-I headquarters staff for help with stratifying the detainees in his custody as low-, medium-, or high-risk. By spring, TF-134 had developed criteria for categorizing the level of security risk each detainee posed. A composite score for each detainee included variables such as

- their disciplinary record inside the detention facility
- their level of military training
- whether they could explain why U.S. forces had detained them
- their interaction with others in small-group discussion settings
- whether they had been part of any *Sharia* courts inside the compounds. (Gardner, 2007)[7]

It took months to stratify and categorize the detainees properly. As the number of detainees grew, Gardner and his staff devised a 1-through-5 scale for detainees, with "5" reserved for the highest-risk detainees. Unfortunately, this scale accounted only for a prisoner's personal history of violence and not for an ability to support or direct others' violence.

The classification and categorization identified nearly 3,000 detainees for whom there was some evidence of criminal activity and a link to the insurgency. Continued rumors about the impending end of U.S. authority to detain Iraqi citizens by 2007 spurred furious efforts to parse out the criminals among the detainee population and convict them in the Central Criminal Court of Iraq (CCCI). In the summer and fall of 2006, TF-134 spent an enormous amount of time and resources working with the CCCI on improving procedures. Still, in many cases charges were dismissed due to incomplete criminal dossiers, as field intelligence required to detain persons differed from criminal evidence needed to convict them. Classification restrictions on intelligence, prohibiting its use in court, also contributed to the inability to gain convictions in many cases. Over time, the difficulties

---

7   These were self-appointed courts dispensing vigilante justice with little or no basis in Islamic practice or real *Sharia* law. For example, prisoners found to be in possession of a photograph of their wife would have their eyelids cut off to punish them for keeping a pictorial image of a woman, which the Salafists believed to be a sin.

in providing necessary evidence for criminal convictions resulted in a decrease in the number of detainees sent to criminal courts, further increasing the overall detainee population.

Understandably, the situation was extremely taxing for the detainees as well. Although TF-134 sought to make the detention process transparent to prisoners, using mechanisms such as an illustrated book to explain the detention process from initial detention to hearing to release, many prisoners believed they were in "detention for life" (Gardner, 2007). Gardner was burdened by the feeling that he was holding too many individuals whose guilt or innocence had not yet been determined. He therefore introduced a Combined Review and Release Board to periodically review prisoner status (see Figure 5.2). Adjudications from this board helped reassure the increasingly frustrated detainee population that their cases were being reviewed. In particular, it helped distinguish third-country nationals, including those

Figure 5.2
U.S. Officials Review a Detainee's File During a Review Committee Board Meeting

SOURCE: Defense Video and Imagery Distribution System, 2008b.
RAND MG934-5.2

from Egypt and Sudan who had merely been working as laborers in Iraq, from foreign fighters.

Counterinsurgency Behind the Wire

By the summer of 2006, Gardner, who was known to roam the compounds at night, believed he had an "information war" on his hands (Gardner, 2007). Administrators also realized that prisoner-on-prisoner violence had become a serious problem. The worst of this violence consisted of "punishments" inflicted on less observant and more-moderate detainees by their Takfiri fellows.[8] Threats and intimidation among prisoners prevented guards and the command from becoming aware of this violence for some time. Once it came to their notice, counterinsurgency teams worked with TIF guards to identify the leaders responsible and to break up the *Sharia* courts that extremists had established within the compounds. The effort to address these problems faced some challenges. Without appropriate precautions, "snitches" and collaborators could be subject to retribution.

Gardner considered placing all detainees in individual cells so as to prevent mutual harm and radicalization, but he realized it would be logistically impossible and might cause objections from organizations such as the Red Cross, because solitary confinement is considered a form of punishment. Instead Gardner used some standard prison procedures to maintain control. Abrupt relocations of detainees helped stanch extremist indoctrination and break up the vigilante *Sharia* courts. One suspected al Qaeda in Iraq operative was moved six times, hampering his recruitment of detainees. Gardner could not place the worst extremists in solitary confinement for extended periods of time (only pending proceedings or serving a sentence), as this was generally prohibited by the Fourth Geneva Convention and too difficult to implement. Nevertheless, holding them in groups of three or four apart from other prisoners did help curb their recruitment efforts (Gardner, 2007).

---

[8]   Takfiris regard their own version of Islam as the only proper one and view those with a more-moderate religious view as not being proper Muslims. They were among the most violent and dangerous detainees.

Gardner instituted a variety of programs that eventually became part of a counterinsurgency strategy behind the wire. The programs had several objectives, including

- identifying and deradicalizing religious extremists
- countering insurgent fervor and recruiting efforts among detainees
- giving detainees hope that there was a process in place to review their cases and they would be treated fairly
- filling the empty hours of detention and relieving the boredom and tension inside the camps—perhaps the most important of all.

Gardner had a bilingual, bicultural advisor (BBA) supervise the introduction of radio and television programming for the inmates. Gardner's staff observed that detainees enjoyed cartoons and action movies, so BBAs provided a selection of these every day. The approach did carry some risks; Gardner and his staff soon discovered that one of the stations broadcasting to detainees was also sending surreptitious messages to them. Yet Gardner and his staff were heartened to discover that the extremists seemed to regard this programming as a threat, for they soon began throwing rocks at the screens that were set outside the fence lines.

Gardner's counterinsurgency teams found that there were 200 teachers among detainees who could provide basic education to others (Figure 5.3). Gardner instituted rudimentary civics classes for detainees in the prerelease process. These classes educated the detainees about the Iraqi constitution, the composition of the Iraqi parliament, and life in a democratic system.

Sunni political leaders, tribal leaders, and clerics were invited regularly to the TIFs to meet with detainees. Political leaders tried to convey the message that the political system had changed, that the detainees could be part of the new Iraq, and that they should cooperate in detention until their release. Tribal leaders similarly sought to reassure detainees that they had not been forgotten, that theirs was a temporary situation, and that they would be able to return to normal life and to familiar society soon. Gardner believed this effort had a

Figure 5.3
Detainees Begin to Educate Other Detainees—Under Task Force
Supervision

SOURCE: TF-134.
RAND *MG934-5.3*

measurable impact on the compounds of moderate detainees at Abu
Ghraib and Camp Cropper (Gardner, 2007).

In conjunction with Iraqi political leaders, Gardner also instituted
a "sponsor program." The idea was to find someone of influence within
the community to take responsibility for the released detainees and
guarantee their good behavior. Unfortunately, this program proved
susceptible to misuse, as influential individuals with ties to militias and
armed groups took advantage of it to have their members released from
custody. With modifications and adjustments, and given improved
conditions following the surge, this program eventually developed into
the more successful "guarantor program," in which persons of authority, such as tribal leaders, gave assurances that individuals released into
their custody would be supervised by them and would not return to
the insurgency.

Gardner also sought, with help from the U.S. Agency for International Development, to obtain jobs in the community for former

detainees in the western Al Anbar province. In Gardner's view, providing an alternative career path for released insurgents and encouraging their reintegration into peaceful mainstream society is an important part of a broader counterinsurgency policy, and assistance with jobs and work opportunities is an important piece of this.

Perhaps the most-ambitious program was aimed at the minority that consisted of religious radicals held in detention. Gardner sought assistance from government agencies to better understand Islamist extremists. The Joint Information Operations Center at Kelly Air Force Base in San Antonio, Texas, informed him of disengagement and deradicalization programs in Singapore and Saudi Arabia. The Saudis declined to work with U.S. detention authorities in Iraq, but personnel in the Singapore program agreed to visit TF-134 headquarters, and in May 2007, Gardner established a pilot program to interview Takfiris, with the ultimate goal of reeducating them.

The religious reeducation program had the potential to be effective with detainees who fit a particular profile: those who were religiously motivated, but not as committed to their radical interpretation of Islam as to be impervious to the opinions of more-moderate religious leaders. These classes, however, were less effective than hoped. Indeed, the classes angered some detainees and increased rather than decreased tension. There were also allegations that the wrong clerics had been selected and that preparation had been insufficient.[9]

Disconnect Between Operational Reality and Official Policy

By January 2007, the United States was preparing for a surge of forces to help break the cycle of sectarian violence that had gripped Iraq. Gardner felt that U.S. detainee policy, oversight, and resourcing processes did not support the operational requirements of the surge (Gardner, 2007). For example, only Congress could authorize contin-

---

[9] Though the RAND team did not investigate this in depth, there were some troubling signs. Just before and during our project team's tenure in Iraq, the religious reeducation program experienced a number of difficulties to which we were privy. At one point, some in TF-134 believed that some of the "moderate" clerics in fact held Salafist views and were using the program to infiltrate the prison population. In another instance, the prisoners became so enraged by efforts to "religiously educate" them that a prison riot resulted.

gency construction, but Congress was reluctant to authorize any construction for detainee operations because it was hoping to hand off detention operations to the Iraqi authorities as soon as possible.

The Office of the Secretary of Defense (OSD) actually reduced funding for detention operations even as the surge approached, providing further evidence that the importance and role of detainee operations were still not recognized. Gardner perceived himself as being consistently obliged to improvise and find workaround solutions. It generally took months for TIF construction initiatives to be approved, even though comparable allocations in wartime were typically approved within weeks.

With the planned surge of more than 20,000 U.S. troops imminent, policymakers finally recognized that increased military operations would likely result in a parallel surge of detainees. Still, the expectations and the suggested policies varied enormously. Gardner projected that his TIFs would need space for 30,000 detainees, and he began to add more buildings to Camps Bucca and Cropper. OSD did not initially provide resources for this construction, insisting that detainees should be handed off to the Iraqis. It later modified that posture and instructed Gardner to prepare for 60,000 to 70,000 detainees (Gardner, 2007). At another extreme, U.S. Senator Jeff Sessions calculated that given the extent of the conflict, Coalition authorities "should be holding 90,000 detainees." In fact, the number of detainees would peak at more than 25,000 in late 2007 (Figure 5.4).

Violence Flares Again

The detainee program in Iraq was bursting at the seams. Difficulty in forecasting the number of detainees necessitated a series of improvisations to provide housing, health care, and food for an expanding population. Overcrowding was a constant concern, limiting the ability to segregate the groups within the camp, leading to frustration among the detainee population, and increasing the risk of violence.

In March and April 2007, several events led to a substantial increase in violence at Camp Bucca (see Figure 5.5). Detainees were disturbed by news of the construction of additional compounds, by a reduction in releases, by the departure of a number of detainees' fami-

Figure 5.4
Total Number of Detainees in Task Force 134 Custody by Month, December 2006 to May 2008

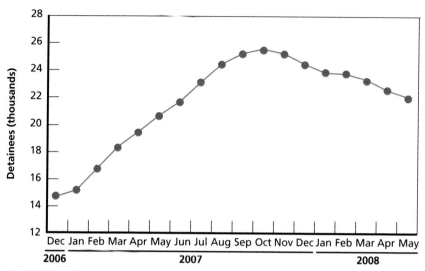

SOURCE: TF-134.
RAND *MG934-5.4*

lies from Baghdad with no forwarding address, and by sheer exhaustion and hopelessness regarding their circumstances. At that point, there were individual detainees who had spent 36 months in detention with no clear hope for release. As a result, many concluded that they had nothing to lose by showing their anger and becoming violent.

Gardner was caught up in a cycle of crisis management. Under those circumstances there was little room for innovation or finding ways to make the detention process a greater part of the counterinsurgency effort. For example, Gardner saw the necessity for, but never actually commissioned, a comprehensive motivation and morale survey.

Figure 5.5
Masked Detainees Charge the Guard Force During Riots at Camp Bucca,
March 2007

SOURCE: TF-134.
RAND *MG934-5.5*

Innovations Under a New Commander[10]

Marine Corps Major General Douglas Stone assumed command of
detainee operations in May 2007 after a three-week overlap between
the commanders. By the time Stone arrived, the number of internment
facilities had been streamlined to three: Camp Bucca, Camp Cropper,
and the Temporary Internment and Protection Camp near Forward
Operating Base Grizzly (which Stone later renamed the Ashraf Refugee Camp). His predecessors had built or received funding for much
of the infrastructure needed for detainee operations, with the issue of
detention capacity resolved for the moment. Stone was able to concen-

---

[10] The overview of detention operations provided this section is based on direct observation
by RAND researchers, as well as extensive interviews with Major General Douglas Stone
(2007 and 2008–2009).

trate on other initiatives. This included closer coordination with Army General David Petraeus, the MNF-I commanding general, as Stone attempted to turn detainee operations from "a strategic risk to a strategic advantage."[11]

A September 2007 internal discussion paper prepared for Stone laid out the following critical challenges facing detention operations:

- developing a legal framework to shape and inform long-term detainee operations, with a sensitive and transparent interpretation of international law being critical to a successful conclusion of detainee operations in Iraq
- matching internment capacity with a detainee population growing at an unprecedented rate. If the current rate of growth were to continue, capacity at both GOI and MNF-I prison and detention facilities would be reached by December 2008
- transferring detainees from MNF-I to GOI authority. This was complicated by doubts about human-rights compliance by the GOI and a 40 percent dismissal rate of Iraqi court hearings.
- Coalition detainees being detained as threats to security but with insufficient evidence to charge them in a court of law
- balancing risk of releasing terrorists against lengthy internment of innocent civilians. Approximately 90 percent of the detainees in MNF-I custody were being released without trial. The length of detention was increasing theatre tensions and creating a strategic risk. However, MNF-I and GOI were unwilling to release possible terrorists. (Bodington, 2007)

These realities shaped Stone's approach to detention operations. Stone described a strategy for detention operations which consisted of (a) knowing the enemy, especially identifying detainees who would never renounce the insurgency, (b) focusing on counterinsurgency rather than corrections, (c) focusing on rehabilitation rather than

---

[11] Part of Stone's motivation for reframing the question of detainee operations was a belief that while Coalition forces had "come to view detainee operations as a risk," insurgents had come "to view them as an opportunity, i.e., a chance to network, train, and plan further operations" (Stone, conversations with RAND researchers, 2007).

warehousing, and (d) developing a coherent release, detention, rule of law, and reintegration perspective.[12] To implement this strategy, Stone focused on identifying irreconcilables; reconciling, rehabilitating, and reintegrating those who would eventually be released; and developing a communication strategy to turn detention operations into a strategic advantage rather than a strategic risk.

Irreconcilables

Stone sought the formal designation of "irreconcilable" for detainees who could not accept the changed circumstances of their country, were likely to return to violence if released, and would therefore require indefinite custody. Such detainees were to be given to Iraqi authorities after the length of time for which Coalition forces could hold them had elapsed. Stone faced a challenge in identifying irreconcilables with some certainty so as to guard against a miscarriage of justice while protecting the future stability of Iraq. Some irreconcilables, such as those caught with weapons and those who confessed on tape to killing Americans, were readily identified, although, in some cases, circumstances could mitigate the level of risk posed by release. Stone hired psychologists and religious scholars to assess the impulses behind the violent behavior. Camp administrators developed and maintained a database of infractions committed during detention and used it to assess a detainee's propensity for violence. Such assessment considered (a) severity of the current offense, (b) prior detention, (c) severity of behavior during detention, (d) number of violent or extremist-related disciplinary reports, (e) age, and (f) social, personal, and environmental characteristics, such as drug use, education, and family stability. The final designation as "irreconcilable" would require multiple reviews by MNF-I review boards.[13]

---

[12]   Stone, email to Cheryl Benard, 2007.

[13]   The MNF-I review boards include both GOI and MNF-I representatives. The process of indentifying and categorizing an individual as irreconcilable was not fully developed at the time RAND researchers left Iraq.

Strategies for Reintegration, Reconciliation, and Counterradicalization

Detainees not considered to be irreconcilables would be released eventually. However, Stone was concerned that the detainee camps had become hotbeds for "jihadists." He initially assumed that a strong motivation of the insurgents, and the logic with which they made their goals resonate with the broader Iraqi audience, was religious. He sought to demonstrate a positive interest in Islam, keeping a Quran on his desk and referring to his reading of it in conversations and interviews. He decided to reintroduce a religious discussion program in the detention facilities.[14]

Subsequent interviews of detainees by TF-134 staff would show religion had been important to a minority of detainees before they reached the camps. But early during his tenure, Stone feared that without a religious education program he would have "20 riots a month" on his hands (Stone, 2007). Over time, Stone saw the religion classes primarily as a means to calm a troubled detainee population by providing them comfort through religion.

By the time Stone took command of detainee operations, some detainees had been imprisoned for several years with no clear timeline or expectations for release. Many were not aware that their cases were periodically reviewed by administrative boards. The detainees' principal grievance was that they did not know what was being done about their situation. In response, Stone instituted more-frequent and formal reviews of the cases against detainees (Figure 5.6). Unlike administrative reviews, the new review process brought the detainee before the review board in person, where he was able to answer questions and tell his side of the story. Stone and his staff attributed the decline in disturbances in the detainee facilities to the institution and demonstration of a fair process and more-frequent detention review boards. Stone felt

---

[14] Gardner introduced and withdrew religious education after resistance to the classes increased tensions among the detainees. We do not know if Stone considered past problems in his plans for religious discussion groups. However, during the RAND team's time in Iraq, we were witness to discussions questioning the credentials of the individuals hired to lead the religious discussion groups and disagreements among the religious teachers stemming from differences between Shia and Sunni interpretations of Islam.

Figure 5.6
A Task Force 134 Board Reviews a Detainee's Case

SOURCE: Defense Video and Imagery Distribution System, 2008a.
RAND *MG934-5.6*

that these review boards, as well as the visible release of some prisoners, who were given a formal and public release ceremony and went home on what prisoners called the "Happy Bus," did much to calm detainees and contributed to better public relations within Iraq and internationally.

Once released, Stone felt that many Iraqis would have a better chance of turning away from the insurgency if they had a sense of hope in the future of Iraq and a trade or skill they could use to support their families. This also applied to the population of Iraqi males who were not in detention but who were unemployed or underemployed. Stone believed that these individuals were at risk to join the insurgency, and a broader counterinsurgency plan should include them as well as those already detained.

To accomplish this goal Stone developed an idea that he called the TIF Reconciliation Centers (TIFRCs). Two centers were planned, one at Taji, the other at Ramadi. The plan was to take recently released detainees and unemployed adult Iraqi males and pay them a small stipend while they received vocational and civic training at the TIFRCs.

Stone believed that teaching detainees skills that they could parlay into employment served several purposes. With salaries and something to do, detainees would be more likely to feel that they had a constructive part in rebuilding their society and be less likely to return to the insurgency. Stone also felt that such a continuing relationship with detainees might yield information about the insurgency. As he said, "jobs will make security more than security will make jobs" (Stone, 2007).

From Strategic Risk to Strategic Advantage

To improve U.S. credibility, Stone also initiated an aggressive and highly nuanced strategic communications effort focused on transparency in detainee operations (Department of Defense, 2007). Stone sought to convey the message that he was presiding over a new era in detainee operations, one distinct from Abu Ghraib. For the first time, a TF-134 commander, often throwing in a few words of Arabic, was attempting to speak directly to the people of Iraq and the region. Stone explained in forthright language why detainees were being held and that determining which detainees committed violence against their fellow Iraqis was not always easy and could result in regrettable but unavoidable delays in release.

Stone's overarching goal was to ensure "transparency in the detainee process" for the detainees, their families, local and foreign publics, and the press. Speaking directly to Iraqi and Middle Eastern audiences through the Arab media was a "revolutionary" step for detainee operations in Iraq (Petraeus, 2008).

The public affairs officers assigned to Stone's command were accustomed to working with the major Western media outlets. They did not have the language skills and connections necessary to reach out to local and regional media outlets. Stone wanted to reach these audiences, so in the fall of 2007 he commissioned the support of an expert on Arab media and public relations. The role of the expert was to help Stone understand what the Arabic-language press was reporting about detention operations and to develop a proactive engagement strategy with these media. By the spring of 2008, TF-134 had managed several successful press conferences with pan-Arab press; organized and managed six delegations of Iraqi press visits to the TIFs and interviews with Major General Stone; arranged for foreign and local press to witness eight detainee release ceremonies (see Figure 5.7), with an impressive turnout; and organized and managed Al-Iraqiya (Iraq), Al Arabiya TV (regional), Al Jazeera English, and Baghdad Satellite TV visits to Camp Cropper.

This comprehensive strategic communications effort allowed Stone to correct misconceptions, reach out to pivotal media, and counter allegations with facts much more effectively. Stone designed a strategic communications campaign that led to

- perceived positive change after Abu Ghraib, with remaining negative coverage limited to past events
- positive reception of reeducation programs
- ample coverage of detainee release.

A June 2008 analysis by TF-134 showed a shift beginning in early 2007, while Gardner was still in command, from sustained nega-

Figure 5.7
A Recently Released Detainee at an Iraqi Police Station

SOURCE: Defense Video and Imagery Distribution System, 2008c.
RAND MG934-5.7

tive media coverage to positive coverage of detainee operations in Iraq in the Western, Middle Eastern, and Iraqi press, demonstrating the benefits of an accessible, energetic outreach effort toward national and regional media.

Special Populations

One of the unique challenges that TF-134 faced as counterinsurgency operations continued, particularly after the surge of U.S. forces, was managing several special populations. As the surge in Iraq increased, Coalition forces began detaining more juveniles (those younger than 18). In January 2007, there were fewer than 300 youth detainees; by the end of the year, mostly as a result of the surge, there were nearly 900 (see Figure 5.8).

Figure 5.8
Number of Detainees 18 Years of Age or Younger by Month, January 2007 to March 2008

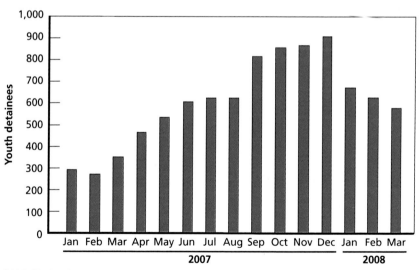

SOURCE: TF-134.
RAND *MG934-5.8*

Initially TF-134 preferred to hand young detainees over to the Iraqi juvenile or criminal court system. The Iraqi courts, however, were inclined to indiscriminately release juveniles, even if they had committed very serious acts. TF-134 therefore found it necessary to keep them in custody. Administrators had housed the worst juvenile offenders at Camp Bucca but soon recognized that this exposed them to the influence of the adult extremists being housed there. Ultimately, the Coalition kept all juvenile detainees at Camp Cropper, eventually segregating them from adults. The difficulties in handling juvenile detainees reflected a lack of doctrine and preparation, forcing the implementers in the field to improvise and to make judgment calls in a volatile and stressful setting. U.S. troops generally felt uncomfortable about capturing and detaining teens, preteens, and children. Yet, given their alleged involvement in placing improvised explosive devices (IEDs) that had killed people, it was not possible to release them.

The reluctance to detain and hold females was even greater. Initially, Coalition forces declined to detain them for three reasons: the risk of any allegations of abuse in the wake of the Abu Ghraib scandal, the fear of a popular backlash, and the administrative difficulties of holding a mixed-gender population. Eventually, several cases of failed female suicide bombers compelled the Coalition to detain a small number of women in a segregated complex where high-value detainees where also housed.

An additional challenge for TF-134 was its task to provide care and custody for about 5,000 members of the Mujahedin-e Khalq (MEK), a heavily armed paramilitary group that had been exiled from Iran and may have been marginally involved in military operations against invading Coalition forces in 2003. The MEK had been designated a Foreign Terrorist Organization by the U.S. State Department in 1997 and was accused of aiding Saddam Hussein's oppression of Iraqi Kurds and Shia. As part of a Special Forces–brokered ceasefire, MEK members were granted protected status under the Fourth Geneva Convention (Goulka et al., 2009). This left U.S. authorities in the difficult position of extending protection to a terrorist group that was not indigenous to Iraq and was no longer welcomed by Iraqi authorities.

Detainee Motivation and Morale

In October 2003, the Secretary of Defense noted

> Today, we lack metrics to know if we are winning or losing the
> global war on terror. Are we capturing, killing or deterring and
> dissuading more terrorists every day than the madrassas and the
> radical clerics are recruiting, training and deploying against us?
> (Rumsfeld, 2003)

Although this observation reflected the specific need to understand more about the network of religiously motivated terrorists, it
highlighted a general need to understand the motivations of our adversaries, whether they be religiously or otherwise driven to act against us.
Other demands for a motivation and morale study followed, including those advocating an examination of broader motivations (Packer,
2006).

The population of detainees, many known to be active participants in the insurgency, presented a valuable fountain of information
that could be used to explore and validate official assumptions. Nevertheless, by May 2007, very little information had been gathered or was
available about the makeup of the detainee population or motivation
for participating in the insurgency.

Instead, the official understanding of the motivations and morale
of the insurgency was largely based on speculation and expert opinion.
For example, it was a commonly held belief among TF-134 personnel
that the detainees were driven to counterinsurgency by religious fervor,
even as it became clear that some of the internal disturbances at the
TIFs were caused by the more-religious minority's efforts to impose
religious observance on the more-secular majority. Stone and other
senior leaders posited that if insurgents were driven by extremist religious rhetoric, they could be "turned around" or "calmed down" if
they only became more educated about the Quran.

Another commonly stated belief for participation in the insurgency was economic. This assumption posited that some insurgents
were motivated to join the insurgency because they had no other way

to support their families; they really did not want to participate in the insurgency, but the survival of their families depended on it.

While assumptions about religious and economic motivations may have been applicable to a subset of the detainees, there was no way to validate the applicability of these assumptions to the broader population of detainees.

Task Force 134 Transition-In Survey

In December 2007, TF-134 began administering a "transition-in" survey to every new detainee arriving at a TIF, and by the spring of 2008, more than 3,000 detainees had completed the survey. The transition-in survey focused on the detainee's socioeconomic background, religious beliefs, and physical and mental well being, with questions on marital status, number of children, income, trade skills, education, previous employment, religious beliefs, and exposure to traumatic events and violence as a result of the war.

The survey was designed to help the task force improve management of detainees, provide better care, and develop improved programs to help with reintegration. One set of questions focused on identifying detainees with potentially serious physical and psychological problems, allowing detention officials to properly house them in the camp and to identify the need for treatment earlier than was possible before the survey. Questions about religion were designed to help identify religious extremists. These questions were indirect and included hypothetical questions on whether Muslims should be compelled to fast during Ramadan or to observe all daily prayers. Extremists tend to consider it their responsibility to enforce compliance of these strictures by their fellow Muslims, while nonextremists, even those with strongly held religious beliefs, will leave to the individual how to behave properly and to God how to punish noncompliance. Further, religious discussion classes at the TIFs were already in place when the transition-in survey was first administered, as were the religious extremists who were trying to convert detainees. Therefore, it was deemed particularly useful to obtain a baseline assessment of the religious beliefs of the detainee population before exposure to the religious influences inside the camps.

The survey also had questions to help the task force design educational and vocational programs that met the needs of the detainees.

Finally, the survey gave the task force another perspective on the views and attitudes of the Iraq population with regard to such important topics as sectarian violence, concerns for the future, and their attitudes toward the Coalition. Similarly, survey results allowed detention officials to assess the validity of commonly held assumptions about the education, religiosity, and economic well-being of the detainees that affected detainee policies, as well as broader policies. Among the assumptions tested using the survey results were that the insurgency was fueled by sectarian hatred, that religious extremism and al Qaeda were behind the insurgency, that economic subsistence was a motive for the insurgency, and that the vast majority of detainees were illiterate, making them easy prey for extremist recruiters.

Transition-In Survey Conclusions

As in previous detainee operations, the task force found differences between what program administrators believed about their charges and what the administrators found about them. This underscores the importance of a survey being a standard component of any conflict yielding prisoners or detainees, and one that should commence with the very first captures. The information and understanding sought by such a survey are essential to understanding any conflict, the circumstances that can help bring it to a conclusion, and the true nature and composition of the adversary. Detainees can also provide insights on the attitudes, values, expectations, and perceptions of the population at large. This includes questions about how neighborhoods and communities are faring, the reasons for community support for an insurgency, and what outcomes would be deemed acceptable by which segments of the population.

Summarizing Changes in Detainee Operations

Those who commanded U.S. detainee operations in Iraq after the end of major combat operations on April 30, 2003, did not fully leverage the lessons of U.S. history in capturing and interning enemy forces. Many of the housing, identification, classification, segregation, and vocational programs they launched were remarkably similar to those attempted repeatedly since World War II, but there was no effort to discern what had or had not worked in these programs, much less any research on how these programs were designed. Indeed, in most cases there were coincidental "reinventions of the wheel," with no knowledge of precedent.

There were a few attempts to learn from past experience. For example, in 2006 when Gardner was contemplating the construction of new compounds at two internment facilities, he asked his staff to review the Koje-do riots of the Korean War (discussed earlier in this work). This research led him to reduce the number of prisoners he intended to hold in the new compounds.

Adding to the challenges of detainee operations were Washington policymakers who had different assumptions than those in Iraq about detention operations. Such assumptions, and perhaps a loss of confidence resulting from the Abu Ghraib scandal, led them to initially underfund detention operations even as U.S. forces surged. Command and control of detainee operations was also split between different command entities, with little "unity of command."

Detainee operations in Iraq reflected the conflicting prior requirements of prosecuting major combat operations and the subsequent requirements of prosecuting a counterinsurgency. By 2004 commanders in Iraq began to recognize that they were not just managing a follow-on phase of major combat operations but a full counterinsurgency. In counterinsurgency operations, it is less obvious to soldiers who are combatants and who are common criminals. In Iraq, many were detained because they were near the target of interest but were later determined to be peripheral to the enemy operation and, therefore, should not have been detained.[15] Nevertheless, in the minds of

---

[15] An Army lieutenant colonel who had been a Detainee Contingency Review Board member told us in July 2007, based on his reviews of more than 300 detainee records, that "95 percent of these guys were in the wrong place at the wrong time."

some ground commanders, temporarily sweeping such detainees from the battlefield was good.

Eventually, MNF-I commanders realized that detention operations provided an opportunity to reeducate and deradicalize detainees prior to their release. Through a strategic media campaign, they sought to turn a strategic risk into a strategic advantage.

The Iraqi detainee operations and Operation Iraqi Freedom experience underscores the need for the United States to develop doctrine for this critical element of conflict. When executed efficiently, detainee operations can make a pivotal contribution to counterinsurgency. If executed incorrectly, detainee operations can fuel the insurgency and erode support for the conflict at home and internationally.

Effective detainee operations can help degrade the enemy's ability to regenerate forces, disrupt his battle rhythm, attack his motivation and morale, and control information about the conflict. The lessons learned in Iraq and earlier conflicts should be leveraged and applied in Afghanistan or any other area where U.S. forces find themselves engaged in traditional or asymmetric warfare.

CHAPTER SIX

Conclusions and Recommendations

U.S. forces have generally treated POW and detainee operations as an afterthought, a perhaps inevitable but largely inconvenient collateral effect of military conflict. Such operations would be better considered as a central part of the successful prosecution of a conflict, particularly a counterinsurgency.

Determining how to gain knowledge from, hold, question, influence, and release captured adversaries ought to be viewed as an important component of military tactics and doctrine. The mechanisms for doing so should be a standard part of any war plan and should evolve as necessary over time. Failure to recognize this has many negative consequences.

The typical pattern of prisoner and detainee operations has included belated recognition of the total number of prisoners that will need to be housed, hasty scrambling for resources, initial crisis management, eventual concerted but difficult efforts to improve operations, and, ultimately, implementation of programs to influence prisoners. This same pattern unfolded in the Iraq conflict.

By analyzing detainee operations in Iraq and documenting the steps that were taken, we have the opportunity to improve doctrine. Our recommendations based on Iraq and historical cases encompass two overarching areas: basic elements of detention operations and doctrinal issues.

Basic Elements of Detention Operations

Detainee operations tend to be large and complex. In World War II, the United States held nearly a half-million German prisoners. In the Korean War, a single camp at Koje-do held more than 100,000 prisoners. In Vietnam and Iraq, U.S. forces dealt with a smaller number of prisoners and detainees but had to satisfy more exacting legal standards for their treatment and adjudication. In Iraq, the authority to detain granted under UNSCR 1546 and managed under the revised CPA Memorandum No. 3 distinguished between security detainees and criminal detainees. Security detainees were to be held temporarily, their cases reviewed periodically, and eventually released back into society. This caused tensions between TF-134 and MNC-I, which viewed releases as putting dangerous insurgents back on the streets. The GOI had mixed views of the detain-and-release policy. At times it found it politically expedient to pressure Coalition forces for mass releases, but it also did not want detainees who were security threats back on the streets. Criminal detainees were to be given to the Iraqi justice system for prosecution. The distinction between security and criminal detainees created two challenges. First, detention authorities needed a way to identify detainees who were irreconcilable and who would return to violent struggle if released. Second, detention authorities had to convince field commanders that their troops needed to gather evidence at the scene that could be used to convict detainees in an Iraqi court. Neither task was easy.

Further complicating the detainee management process were special populations, such as women and juveniles, who had to be housed separately from the male adults, and, in the case of the juveniles, provided basic education.

Future engagements are bound to present their own unique characteristics. Nevertheless, it is reasonable to construct guidance and doctrine around a basic model including the elements below.

Basic Care and Custody of Detainees

The United States must plan and provide for the care of detainees in its custody, and it must do so prior to their detention. In World

War II, the United States had not anticipated having a half-million German soldiers in its custody and did not know how best to assure order among them. In Korea, allied forces had not anticipated the need for a virtual city for detainees. In Iraq, though the number of detainees was smaller, it increased both progressively and, at times, sharply, and failures within the operation unfolded in the spotlight of international attention. During the surge, resources for detainee operations did not increase at the same pace as captures, making it necessary to improvise. Rather than working through DoD channels, senior Army officers in command of detainee operations often had to go outside the Army chain of command to acquire the resources necessary to fulfill their responsibilities. These examples show that accurately forecasting the numbers of prisoners that a military engagement will yield is a difficult endeavor. Therefore, a flexible holding and administration system should be devised. It should

- be capable of being rolled out quickly for varying numbers of persons
- be able to conform to differing configurations, depending on whether subgroups need to be segregated
- have available basic programs for informing and managing the prisoners, such as the posters TF-134 staff created to inform detainees of rules
- give commanders basic, adaptable tools for holding, housing, and managing detainees and prisoners.

Planning for Special Populations

Future operations are more likely to have special populations of detainees. Three such populations in Iraq were juveniles, women, and religious extremists. The presence of juveniles, whose numbers nearly reached 1,000, required Coalition forces to operate separate facilities housing them as well as to provide programs by which they could continue their education. Similarly, though initially reluctant to detain women, in large part because of the fear of a popular backlash, several cases of failed suicide bombings by women forced the Coalition to establish a small, separate detention facility for women. Finally, addressing the threat posed by members of the MEK forced the Coalition to extend protections to a group neither indigenous to Iraq nor welcomed by Iraqi authorities.

The presence of these special populations among those under custodial care by TF-134 required special planning, application of scarce resources, and political considerations. Existing and future operations would benefit from applying the lessons learned from TF-134's management of these special populations as it develops doctrine and policies for handling detainees and criminals who do not neatly fit into the standard categories of detainees expected in a combat environment.

Gathering Information from Detainees

Besides removing adversaries from the battlefield, detention of soldiers and insurgents can yield information on enemy operations, including planned attacks, size of force, leadership, and resources. Interrogation strategies should reflect the population one expects to hold and the nature of the conflict and should evolve as the conflict evolves.

Initial interrogation focuses heavily on time-sensitive operational information. However, this should not happen at the expense of sociological information that could shed light on the demographics, attitudes, values, support structures, and recruitment of insurgents. On capturing a suspected extremist, often during an ongoing street battle or in the immediate aftermath of an IED attack, soldiers do not have the leisure to ask more than the most pressing questions that would enable them to assess the situation and determine whether to hold that individual. The more-general questions, referred to as "atmospherics" by the military, were contained in the original list of questions but were almost always omitted. The consequence, however, was that often they were not later asked. We recommend restoring these sociological questions, pertaining to education levels, family situation, living circumstances, and professional qualifications, as soon as possible after initial capture and information gathering. When collected properly, this information may be used to design reintegration programs and is helpful in understanding the broader societal context in which troops are operating. It can also facilitate interrogations because it establishes rapport and allows the questioned individual to place his actions in a subjective context.

Developing a Broader Understanding of the Operating Environment
Detainee operations should include an early and comprehensive study to calibrate counterinsurgency operations, discern enemy motivations, and inform programs to counter prevailing mindsets. In the absence of such a study, the United States did not realize that most of the German soldiers it held during World War II were not committed Nazis. Nor, in Korea, did the United States realize that many of its prisoners would not want to return "home."

In Iraq, U.S. forces at first assumed that poverty (economic subsistence) and religious extremism were the primary motivations of insurgents. They designed battlefield strategies and detainee programs accordingly. As later surveys revealed, infusions of cash into troubled areas in many cases just provided an additional source of income for opportunistic, not impoverished, criminals or insurgents. Adequate understanding of the detainee population through an early survey would have led to more-effective initial counterinsurgency operations.

From World War II through Iraq, a better understanding of the detainee population and how its motivations differed by cultural, sociological, political, and economic characteristics would have allowed timely separation of subgroups and prevented unfortunate occurrences of violence within detainee populations. Lack of understanding of differences among prisoner and detainee populations led to grouping together those who should have been kept apart, permitting extremists to perpetrate violence against others as well as to recruit and intimidate their fellow detainees.

Risk Assessment
For reasons of fairness, as well as to avoid the public resentment and the costs associated with detaining innocent persons, it is important to have a good way of assessing the danger an individual may pose if released. There are multiple practical situations that require administrators to make such an assessment on relatively short notice. First, the threat that detainees can pose to each other makes it important to seg-

regate those who are the most extreme and violent. This can reduce the risks of violence, escalation, and recruitment inside the facility. Second, detention administrators may find it necessary to release or hand over a relatively large number of detainees on short notice.

To streamline risk assessment, two steps should be taken. First, each detainee should have a comprehensive file. In Iraq, information about detainees was stored in separate databases. Second, criteria for assessing threats should be developed early. Some of these can be generic and provided to detainee administrators at the start of their mission. Others will be specific to a particular population. In Iraq, the "report cards" used to monitor the conduct of individuals while in detention would have been amenable to a generic template, while the need to identify Salafists/Takfiris and separate them from secular Ba'athists and mainstream religious Iraqis would have required a more-specific template. Future detainee operations should develop databases to assist in proper grouping of prisoners and to release detainees who pose the lowest security threat first.

Feedback Tools

Prisoner and detainee programs will invariably require ongoing adjustments as situations change and as learning occurs. Ongoing adjustments, in turn, will require a set of mechanisms to monitor programs. At present, there is a tendency to institute programs without any mechanism to end or transform them if new facts prove them to be irrelevant or inappropriate.

Detainee authorities presently judge the effectiveness of programs in amorphous ways, such as whether participants show compliance or whether a program leads to a lower number of disturbances. Such metrics neglect the key goal of preparing detainees for release without subsequently joining the insurgency. While compliance and participation may seem desirable in the short run, these may actually reflect a mindset that detainee operations need to counteract. Ideally, detainees will learn civic responsibility and critical thinking, will use these skills upon release, and will not blindly obey whomever is in charge at any given moment, be it Saddam, the insurgency, or even the U.S. military.

Release and Tracking Plan

The U.S. military expends significant resources in capturing and detaining enemy soldiers and insurgents, as well as in providing them with care and education. Yet surprisingly little (or no) effort goes into tracking detainees upon release. In Vietnam, the failure to monitor prisoners and detainees upon release led to concern that programs were doing little but offering participants a respite before they rejoined the fight. In Iraq in 2008, some detainees were being released to family members under a guarantor program. Others were still being unceremoniously returned to their last known location prior to detention or just let go at the gate. Developing a better release system is important, and so is a tracking plan that would allow authorities to calculate recidivism, determine the ebb and flow of the insurgency, and measure the effectiveness of prisoner and detainee programs.

Strategic Communications

The enormous fallout in the wake of past prisoner and detainee scandals illustrates the need for a strategic communications plan (in addition to institutional safeguards against any recurrence of such abuses). A strategic communications plan should not only react to bad news but should also be proactive, providing information and shaping awareness about detainee operations. Such a plan should seek to illuminate through local or regional media innovative detention programs and how these support broader goals. Above all it should create transparency in the detention process and ameliorate concerns of conspiracy and secrecy. Such a plan should address multiple audiences. In Iraq, these included the prisoners and detainees themselves, their families and communities, the Iraqi public, Iraqi officials, regional audiences and officials, Arab and Islamic audiences, European audiences and policymakers, U.S. politicians, and the U.S. public.

Doctrine

The recent U.S. Army (2006b) field manual on counterinsurgency filled a gap but gave little attention to detention operations as a core element of strategy. In Iraq, doctrinal shortcomings regarding detainee operations contributed to a climate that may have fed into the Abu Ghraib scandal. Developing a comprehensive doctrine regarding detainee operations can help ensure their proper functioning within a broader counterinsurgency strategy.

Understanding Legal Requirements of Detention

Legal considerations so dominated Iraqi detention operations, particularly in the initial period, that one frustrated TF-134 Judge Advocate General official described counterinsurgency as "evidentiary warfare." Many of the challenges in Iraqi detainee operations reflected uncertainties about legal considerations and limitations. The legal framework is complicated, and it shapes detention policy and strategy more than any other variable. Determining the proper international conventions to apply and how to apply them was basic to prisoner and detainee operations in Iraq, Vietnam, Korea, and World War II. New international standards are needed for the current era of asymmetric conflict.

In the meantime, detainee administrators are obliged to improvise. In Iraq, the inconsistency of application and process (such as the lack of an accepted legal review process) led to confusion over how to best handle prisoners and even to disturbances in detention camps. Clear legal guidance to detainee administrators and staff judge advocates would help.

There should also be an understanding that some detainees will be prosecuted under military or local civilian law. The soldiers who initially capture and detain individuals are not usually trained in law enforcement. Accordingly, commanders, staff judge advocates, and authorities should work together to enable warfighters to understand the appropriate evidence rules so that when they capture and detain individuals, they can collect the evidence necessary for prosecution (if security conditions permit). In Iraq, this need was recognized late, and many individuals could not be prosecuted for lack of evidence.

Establishing Detainee Operations as an Important Element of Counterinsurgency

Predeployment training exercises and detainee facilities must emphasize that detainee operations are important to counterinsurgency. This is particularly important in the training of guards, who otherwise tend to view their task as mundane and not essential to the counterinsurgency. The lack of understanding of the importance of detainee operations to counterinsurgency has been evident at both tactical and strategic levels. In Iraq, for example, detention authorities had to scrounge for resources to support innovative programs designed to address battlefield realities, while Washington policymakers continued to press for the transfer of detention operations to Iraqi authorities long before this was reasonable.

Developing and Updating Doctrine

The start of a military conflict is not the time to discover that doctrine is woefully inadequate or missing. While detainee operations must be flexible, they require continuously updated doctrine with sufficiently detailed guidance on how to hold and release prisoners, the most-effective means of synchronizing detention and operational strategies and practices, and how to implement key programs and approaches. Policymakers, planners, and operators require an established body of knowledge on detention operations on which to base their initial efforts and from which they can tailor their efforts to the circumstances they face. In recent conflicts, U.S. authorities have often repeated ineffective practices of their predecessors. The United States must develop a more-sustained effort to collect and impart lessons learned from previous efforts and use those to rapidly develop or update doctrine.

Implementing the Most-Effective Approach

Detention operations often implement the most-convenient approach, rather than one best serving an end-to-end process. Detention authorities and military commanders should develop means to assess the most-appropriate approach for their situation, e.g., detain as many or as few as possible and "detain with purpose."

Establishing Detention Responsibilities

Civilian and military authorities should come to an agreement regarding who is in charge from the first day. If different parties are in charge of different aspects of detention, then coordinating and communicating their actions will be essential. In Iraq, policymakers in Washington were in charge of providing the resources to establish and operate detention facilities, battlefield commanders were in charge of establishing guidance on who should be detained and for carrying out the detentions, and TIFs were in charge of housing and releasing detainees. Divided responsibilities are not necessarily a problem, but they can be, e.g., if battlefield commanders believe more persons should be detained than TIF administrators have resources to house.

Identifying Goals

All detention authorities, both military and civilian, should work together to ensure that they have a common understanding of the goal and a common plan for achieving it. In Iraq, intentions vacillated between turning detention operations over to Iraqi authorities and preparing detention capacity for the surge. Such lack of vision for detention operations reflected in many ways the lack of proper development of doctrine and capabilities for detainee operations.

The Legal Source of MNF-I's Authority to Intern for Security Reasons

The legal basis for detention in Iraq shifted following Iraq's reemergence as a sovereign nation on June 28, 2004. Promulgated shortly before the dissolution of the CPA and the reassertion of Iraq's sovereignty, the UN Security Council issued UNSCR 1546 on June 8, 2004, codifying an agreement between the United States, the Interim Iraqi Government (IIG), and the UN Security Council that transformed the nature of Coalition forces' presence in Iraq from invader and occupier to requested force multiplier.

Although the Geneva Conventions had applied in full since the launch of Operation Iraqi Freedom, the Conventions' application changed when UNSCR 1546 deemed the occupation to end with the transfer of power from the CPA to the IIG. The end of the occupation meant that there was no longer a conflict of international character, which in turn meant that the bulk of the Geneva Conventions were no longer legally applicable in Iraq. Instead, the body of law applicable to noninternational armed conflicts applied, which includes Article 3 common to the Geneva Conventions, customary international humanitarian law, and international human rights law (Dörmann and Colassis, 2004). The legal basis of U.S. activity in Iraq following the transfer of power to the IIG was at the invitation of the IIG and was approved by the UN Security Council under its powers provided by Chapter VII of the UN Charter.

The Coalition presence in Iraq was reorganized pursuant to UNSCR 1546, seeing the dissolution of the CPA and its military arm

(Combined Joint Task Force 7) and its replacement by a permanent U.S. Embassy, the newly formed MNF-I, and the warfighting MNC-I.

The specifics of the Coalition's authority were detailed in letters attached to UNSCR 1546 from Prime Minister Dr. Ayad Allawi and Secretary of State Colin Powell. Dr. Allawi requested the MNF-I to retain its presence "to continue efforts to contribute to the maintenance of security and stability in Iraq" (p. 2). On this basis, the Security Council granted the Coalition "the authority to take all necessary measures to contribute to the maintenance of security and stability in Iraq . . . by preventing and deterring terrorism . . ." (paragraph 10, p. 4).[1] According to Secretary Powell, MNF-I's "activities necessary to counter ongoing security threats posed by forces seeking to influence Iraq's political future through violence" included an array of responsibilities, such as "combat operations against members of these groups, *internment where this is necessary for imperative reasons of security*, and the continued search for and securing of weapons that threaten Iraq's security" (p. 12, emphasis added).

Under this new authority, MNF-I was therefore given control over detention operations and was also tasked with ensuring due process and helping Iraq rebuild its judicial, correctional, and law enforcement system. Within MNF-I, TF-134 would assume direct control over detainee operations.

Exactly what rules TF-134 had to implement were not made very clear by UNSCR 1546. The phrase used in Sec. Powell's letter—authorizing internment where "necessary for imperative reasons of security"—comes from the Fourth Geneva Convention, which addresses the treatment of civilians in wartime. Specifically, it comes from Article 78, which states that "[i]f the Occupying Power considers it necessary, for imperative reasons of security, to take safety measures concerning protected persons, it may, at the most, subject them to assigned residence or to internment." Yet, as stated above, only Article 3 applied as a matter of law to conflicts not of an international character, and

---

[1]   MNF-I's authority is subject to review every 12 months or upon request of the GOI and may be terminated at any time upon the request of the GOI (para. 12, p. 4). It has been renewed by Resolutions 1637 (2005), 1723 (2006), and 1790 (2007).

UNSCR 1546 specifically stated that the occupation ended with the creation of the IIG. Other sources of law, such as customary international humanitarian law and international human rights law, did not fill this gap, as customary international humanitarian law suggests that security internment is legal but does not provide its thresholds (Henckaerts, 2005), and international human rights law may forbid it (International Committee of the Red Cross, 2007).

Prior to its dissolution, the CPA addressed this issue by revising CPA Memorandum No. 3 to apply the Fourth Geneva Convention to future detainee operations as a matter of policy—not as a matter of law: "the relevant and appropriate standards set out in the Fourth Geneva Convention . . . shall be applied by the MNF as a matter of policy in accordance with its mandate" (Sec. 1[1][d]). This rule stayed in effect as law within Iraq after the dissolution of the CPA pursuant to CPA Order No. 100.

The CPA memorandum provided a review process for "[a]ny person who is detained by a national contingent of the MNF for imperative reasons of security in accordance with the mandate set out in UNSCR 1546" (Sec. 6[1]). Such persons were classified as "security internees" rather than criminal detainees (Sec. 5[1]). Unlike security internees, criminal detainees "shall be handed over to Iraqi authorities as soon as reasonably practicable" except "at the request of appropriate Iraqi authorities based on security or capacity considerations" (Sec. 5[1]).

Although some commentators saw this as a clear basis for authority to detain,[2] differing interpretations on the limits to that authority arose along with concerns about detaining and releasing individuals who did not meet legal thresholds for retention. For example, many soldiers and Marines viscerally questioned the release of some detainees, who in their view would begin or continue to fight once released from Coalition custody. This tension regarding the decision to release or retain individuals remained a continual subject of debate in Iraq and foreshadows some of the reasons why it was often difficult for tactical and detainee operational planners to coordinate with each other.

---

[2]   On this basis, Chatham House (2006) characterizes "[t]he legal basis for the Coalition security detainees [as] clear and comprehensive."

Bibliography

Andradé, Dale, *Ashes to Ashes: The Phoenix Program and the Vietnam War*, Lexington, Mass.: Lexington Books, 1990.

Ansbacher, Hans, "Attitudes of German Prisoners of War: A Study of the Dynamics of National-Socialistic Followership," *Psychological Monographs*, No. 288, 1948.

Billinger, Robert D., Jr., *Hitler's Soldiers in the Sunshine State: German POWs in Florida*, Gainesville, Fla.: University Press of Florida, 2000.

Bodington, R. H, "MNF-I Long Term Detainee Policy—Discussion Paper," MNF-I internal document, September 2, 2007.

Brandenburg, William, interview with Edward O'Connell, Fort Shafter, Hawaii, June 13, 2007.

Bromley, Dorothy Dunbar, "War Prisoners Include Nazis and Anti-Nazis," *New York Herald Tribune*, April 12, 1944.

Chatham House, "Treatment of Detainees in Iraq," September 28, 2006. As of June 24, 2010:
http://www.chathamhouse.org.uk/files/3361_il280906.pdf

Church, Albert T. III, "Review of Department of Defense Detention Operations and Detainee Interrogation Techniques—Executive Summary," March 11, 2005. As of June 22, 2010:
http://www.defense.gov/news/Mar2005/d20050310exe.pdf

Coalition Provisional Authority, Memorandum Number Three (Revised), Criminal Procedures, June 27, 2004. As of October 4, 2010:
http://www.iraqcoalition.org/regulations/20040627_CPAMEMO_3_Criminal_Procedures__Rev_.pdf

CPA—*See* Coalition Provisional Authority.

Davison, W. Phillips, *User's Guide to the Rand Interviews in Vietnam*, Santa Monica, Calif.: RAND Corporation, R-1024-ARPA, 1972. As of June 21, 2010:
http://www.rand.org/pubs/reports/R1024.html

Defense Video and Imagery Distribution System, "Images: Judicial Pledge Program (Image 1 of 3)," photo ID 72462, taken January 10, 2008a. As of March 11, 2011:
http://www.dvidshub.net/image/72642/judicial-pledge-program

Defense Video and Imagery Distribution System, "Images: Questioning of a Detainee (Image 1 of 3)," photo ID 91427, taken March 3, 2008b. As of March 11, 2011:
http://www.dvidshub.net/image/91427/questioning-detainee

Defense Video and Imagery Distribution System, "Images: Release of Detainees in Iraq (Image 2 of 7)," photo ID 97774, taken March 19, 2008c. As of March 11, 2011:
http://www.dvidshub.net/image/97774/release-detainees-iraq

Department of Defense, Bloggers Roundtable with General Douglas Stone, September 18, 2007. As of June 24, 2010:
http://www.defenselink.mil/dodcmshare/BloggerAssets/2007-09/091807Stone_transcript.pdf

———, Enemy Prisoners of War and Other Detainees, DoD Directive 2310.1, 1994.

Donahue, J. David, "A Civilian Corrections Perspective," Department of the Army, December 20, 2007.

Dörmann, Knut, and Laurent Colassis, "International Humanitarian Law in the Iraq Conflict," German Yearbook of International Law, Vol. 47, 2004, pp. 293–342.

Fourth Geneva Convention—See Geneva Convention Relative to the Protection of Civilian Persons in Time of War.

Gardner, John D., interviews with Cheryl Benard and Edward O'Connell at U.S. Army Europe Headquarters, Heidelberg, Germany, June 2007.

Gebhardt, James F., "The Road to Abu Ghraib: U.S. Army Detainee Doctrine and Experience," Global War on Terrorism Occasional Paper 6, Fort Leavenworth, Kan.: Combat Studies Institute Press, 2005. As of June 24, 2010:
http://cgsc.leavenworth.army.mil/carl/download/csipubs/gebhardt_road.pdf

Geneva Convention Relative to the Treatment of Prisoners of War, July 27, 1929. As of June 18, 2010:
http://www.icrc.org/ihl.nsf/FULL/305?OpenDocument

Geneva Convention Relative to the Treatment of Prisoners of War, August 12, 1949. As of June 18, 2010:
http://www.mineaction.org/downloads/Emine%20Policy%20Pages/Geneva%20Conventions/Geneva%20Convention%20III.pdf

Geneva Convention Relative to the Protection of Civilian Persons in Time of War, August 12, 1949. As of June 18, 2010:
http://www.mineaction.org/downloads/Emine%20Policy%20Pages/Geneva%20Conventions/Geneva%20Convention%20IV.pdf

Goulka, Jeremiah, Lydia Hansell, Elizabeth Wilke, and Judith Larson, *The Mujahedin-e Khalq in Iraq: A Policy Conundrum*, Santa Monica, Calif.: RAND Corporation, MG-871-OSD, 2009. As of June 24, 2010:
http://www.rand.org/pubs/monographs/MG871.html

Greenberg, Lawrence M., *The Hukbalahap Insurrection: A Case Study of a Successful Anti-Insurgency Operation in the Philippines, 1946–1955*, Washington, D.C.: U.S. Army Center of Military History, 1987. As of June 24, 2010:
http://www.history.army.mil/books/coldwar/huk/huk-fm.htm

Henckaerts, Jean-Marie, "Study on Customary International Humanitarian Law: A Contribution to the Understanding and Respect for the Rule of Law in Armed Conflict," *International Review of the Red Cross*, Vol. 87, No. 857, March 2005, pp. 175–212. As of June 24, 2010:
http://www.icrc.org/Web/eng/siteeng0.nsf/htmlall/review-857-p175/$File/irrc_857_Henckaerts.pdf

Hermes, Walter G., *Truce Tent and Fighting Front*, Washington, D.C.: U.S. Army Center of Military History, 1988. As of June 24, 2010:
http://www.history.army.mil/books/korea/truce/fm.htm

Hersh, Seymour M., "Torture at Abu Ghraib," *The New Yorker*, May 10, 2004. As of June 24, 2010:
http://www.newyorker.com/archive/2004/05/10/040510fa_fact

Hunt, David, "Villagers at War: The National Liberation Front in My Tho Province, 1965–1967," *Radical America*, Vol. 8, Nos. 1–2, January–April 1974, pp. 161–171.

Hunt, Richard A., *Pacification: The American Struggle for Vietnam's Hearts and Minds*, Boulder, Colo.: Westview Press, 1998.

International Committee of the Red Cross, "International Humanitarian Law and the Challenges of Contemporary Armed Conflicts," *International Review of the Red Cross*, Vol. 89, No. 867, September 2007, pp. 719–757. As of June 24, 2010:
http://www.icrc.org/Web/eng/siteeng0.nsf/htmlall/review-867-p719/$File/irrc-867-IHL-Challenges.pdf

Joint Chiefs of Staff, *Detainee Operations*, Joint Publication 3-63, May 30, 2008.

Jones, Anthony R., and George R. Fay, *Executive Summary—Investigation of Intelligence Activities at Abu Ghraib*, August 23, 2004.

Kellen, Konrad, *Conversations with Enemy Soldiers in Late 1968/Early 1969: A Study of Motivation and Morale*, Santa Monica, Calif.: RAND Corporation, RM-6131-1-ISA/ARPA, September 1970. As of June 21, 2010:
http://www.rand.org/pubs/research_memoranda/RM6131-1.html

Koch, Jeanette A., *The Chieu Hoi Program in South Vietnam, 1963–1971*, Santa Monica, Calif.: RAND Corporation, R-1172-ARPA, January 1973. As of June 24, 2010:
http://www.rand.org/pubs/reports/R1172.html

Koop, Allen V., *Stark Decency: German Prisoners of War in a New England Village*, Hanover, N.H.: University Press of New England, 1988.

Krammer, Arnold, *Nazi Prisoners of War in America*, Lanham, Md.: Scarborough House, 1979.

Krepinevich, Andrew F., *The Army and Vietnam*, Baltimore: Johns Hopkins University Press, 1986.

Landau, David, "The Viet Cong Motivation and Morale Project," *Ramparts*, November 1972.

Long, Austin, *On "Other War": Lessons from Five Decades of RAND Counterinsurgency Research*, Santa Monica, Calif.: RAND Corporation, MG-482-OSD, 2006. As of June 24, 2010:
http://www.rand.org/pubs/monographs/MG482.html

Marquis, Jefferson P., "The Other Warriors: American Social Science and Nation Building in Vietnam," *Diplomatic History*, Vol. 24, No. 1, Winter 2000, pp. 79–105.

Mayer, Jane, *The Dark Side: The Inside Story of How the War on Terror Turned into a War on American Ideals*, New York: Doubleday, 2008.

Miller, Judith, "Iraqi Militants Becoming Citizens," *Reader's Digest*, July 2008. As of June 24, 2010:
http://www.rd.com/your-america-inspiring-people-and-stories/
iraqi-militants-becoming-citizens/article76144.html

Multi-National Force–Iraq, Commander's COIN Guidance, "Anaconda Strategy Versus al-Qaida in Iraq," July 15, 2008.

O'Connell, Edward, "A Future Beyond a Funeral," *Washington Post*, August 5, 2005, p. A. 15.

Office of the Inspector General, Department of Defense, "Review of DoD-Directed Investigations of Detainee Abuse," August 25, 2006.

Packer, George, "Knowing the Enemy," *The New Yorker*, December 18, 2006. As of June 24, 2010:
http://www.newyorker.com/archive/2006/12/18/061218fa_fact2

Peak, Helen, "Observations on the Characteristics and Distribution of German Nazis," *Psychological Monographs*, No. 276, 1945.

Petraeus, David, interview with Edward O'Connell and Tom Fisher, Camp Victory, Baghdad, April 5, 2008.

Pictet, Jean S., ed., *Commentary: III Geneva Convention Relative to the Treatment of Prisoners of War*, Geneva: International Committee of the Red Cross, 1960. As of June 18, 2010:
http://www.loc.gov/rr/frd/Military_Law/pdf/GC_1949-III.pdf

Prugh, George S., *Law at War: Vietnam 1964–1973*, Washington, D.C.: Department of the Army, 1975. As of June 24, 2010:
http://www.history.army.mil/books/Vietnam/Law-War/law-fm.htm

Robin, Ron, *The Barbed Wire College: Reeducating German POWs in the United States During World War II*, Princeton, N.J.: Princeton University Press, 1995.

Rumsfeld, Donald, "Global War on Terrorism," memorandum to Dick Myers, Paul Wolfowitz, Pete Pace, and Doug Feith, October 16, 2003. As of June 24, 2010:
http://www.usatoday.com/news/washington/executive/rumsfeld-memo.htm

Russo, Anthony, "Looking Backward: Rand and Vietnam in Retrospect," *Ramparts*, Vol. 11, No. 5, November 1972, pp. 40–59.

Schlesinger, James R., et al., *Final Report of the Independent Panel to Review DoD Detention Operations*, Arlington, Va., August 24, 2004. As of June 22, 2010:
http://www.defense.gov/news/Aug2004/d20040824finalreport.pdf

Shanker, Thom, "With Troop Rise, Iraqi Detainees Soar in Number," *New York Times*, August 25, 2007. As of June 24, 2010:
http://www.nytimes.com/2007/08/25/world/middleeast/25detain.html?_r=1&scp=1&sq=thom%20shanker%20troop%20rise%20iraqi%20detainees%20soar%20number&st=cse

Shils, Edward A., and Morris Janowitz, "Cohesion and Disintegration in the Wehrmacht in World War II," *Public Opinion Quarterly*, Vol. 12, No. 2, Summer 1948, pp. 280–315.

Smith, Arthur L., *The War for the German Mind: Re-educating Hitler's Soldiers*, Providence, R.I.: Berghahn Books, 1996.

Stone, Douglas, videotaped interviews with Rebecca BouChebel, Camp Victory, Baghdad, Iraq, November 2008–April 2009.

———, email to Cheryl Benard, 2007.

Summers, Harry G., Jr., *Korean War Almanac*, New York: Facts on File, Inc., 1990.

Third Geneva Convention—*See* Geneva Convention Relative to the Treatment of Prisoners of War.

United Nations Security Council Resolution 1546, the situation between Iraq and Kuwait, June 8, 2004.

United Nations Security Council Resolution 1637, the situation concerning Iraq, November 8, 2005.

United Nations Security Council Resolution 1723, the situation concerning Iraq, November 28, 2006.

United Nations Security Council Resolution 1790, the situation concerning Iraq, December 18, 2007.

UNSCR—*see* United Nations Security Council Resolution.

U.S. Army, *Enemy Prisoners of War, Retained Personnel, Civilian Internees and Other Detainees*, Military Police Regulation 190-8, October 1, 1997.

———, *Military Police Internment—Resettlement Operations*, Field Manual 3-19.40, August 2001.

———, *Counterinsurgency Operations*, Field Manual—Interim 3-07.22, Appendix I: *Planning for Detainee Operations and Field Processing of Detainees*, October 2004.

———, *Command and Control of Detainee Operations*, Field Manual—Interim 3-63.6, September 2005.

———, *Human Intelligence Collector Operations*, Field Manual 2-22.3, September 9, 2006a.

———, *Counterinsurgency*, Field Manual 3-24, December 2006b.

U.S. Army Pacific Headquarters, "The Handling of Prisoners of War During the Korean War," June 1960.

U.S. Senate Committee on Foreign Relations, *Geneva Conventions for the Protection of War Victims*, Washington, D.C.: U.S. Government Printing Office, 1955. As of June 18, 2010:
http://www.loc.gov/rr/frd/Military_Law/pdf/GC-senReport.pdf

U.S. Senate Committee on the Judiciary, *Communist Treatment of Prisoners of War: A Historical Survey*, Washington, D.C.: U.S. Government Printing Office, 1972. As of June 22, 2010:
http://www.loc.gov/rr/frd/Military_Law/pdf/comm_treat_POW.pdf

White, William Lindsey, *The Captives of Korea: An Unofficial White Paper on the Treatment of War Prisoners*, New York: Charles Scribner's Sons, 1957.